LEARN
ENGLISH THE
ICE CREAM WAY

LEARN
ENGLISH THE
ICE CREAM WAY
EASY, ENJOYABLE, AND MEMORABLE

SHALOM KUMAR SIGWORTH

PARTRIDGE
A Penguin Random House Company

To order additional copies of this book, contact
Partridge India
000 800 10062 62
orders.india@partridgepublishing.com

www.partridgepublishing.com/india

CONTENTS

PART IV
ENGLISH COMMUNICATION

To the World's Government leaders, teachers, parents, and students who are struggling to solve English-learning problems

PREFACE

If you want to build a ship, don't drum the men to gather woods, divide the work and give orders. Instead, teach them to yearn for the vast and endless sea.

—Antoine de Saint-Exupéry

Hello! I'm Sigworth.

I'm the author of this innovative book, and I'm glad that my book is in your hands now. This is not just another boring book on grammar. This book takes away the dullness of grammar by putting a lot of flavor and color to the grammar so that the grammar becomes easy and fun. Although the book is addressed to the World's Government leaders, parents, teachers, and students (because all of them are struggling to solve English-learning problems one way or the other), it is written especially for youngsters. It deals with your struggles, problems, and barriers to English learning. This book is based on "ice cream" theme to get you stirred up and learn English in an easy, enjoyable, and memorable way.

My job, as the author of this book, is to make you yearn for a great life. A rich life awaits those who master English. If I mention "grammar", most of you will run away. What if I could tell you that there are huge benefits of learning English? You can become a multimillionaire or a business tycoon; you can walk in the Hollywood Hall of Fame; you can become an author, a Public speaker, or a sought-after Vocalist. You can be involved in Disney productions or Discovery Channel or can become an acclaimed scientist.

You can become a Disk Jockey, a TV host, an eloquent News reporter, or you may work for the World-famous Shakespeare drama company. Well, mastering English language could open doors to all of these, and much more.

This book has a lot of attractive illustrations, icons (ice creams), and signposts (indication of the part of grammar) to guide you through the otherwise bland mass of texts. It also has quite a big number of quotations from eminent people to help you reflect, understand, and change your perspective toward English learning, and get ahead in life. This book is based on one central theme: How to learn English in an easy, enjoyable, and memorable way? The answer is to learn it the ice cream way. Well, you may ask, what do English and ice creams have in common?

First of all, making ice creams is simple: you have to mix some ingredients in certain proportions or quantities and keep them. English communication too is simple. All you have to do is mix some words in a certain order and express them—via writing or speaking.

Second, the success of ice cream making lies in the basics: using the right proportion of ingredients, the right method of mixing them, the right amount of flavoring, and whipping the cream well. Success in English communication also lies in the basics. Learn words; learn grammar; mix words to form phrases, clauses, sentences, and paragraphs—the composite units of communication.

Third, the most interesting aspect in ice cream making is flavoring the ice creams. You can use natural or artificial flavors. According to Paul Gayler, the executive chef at The

Lanesborough in London, a huge variety of things can be used for flavoring the ice creams. Spices, herbs, orange peels, lemon peels, chilies (UK English: chillies), sweetcorn (US English: corn), pepper corn, fruits, dry fruits, baked fruits, grilled fruits, goat cheese, butter milk, coconut milk, tomatoes, Gin, rum, yogurt, bread crumbs, olives, and filo pastry are some of the staggering amount of ingredients that flavors great ice creams. Similarly, flavor or color in English communication can be brought by using the right kind of words. The adjectives are generally used to bring flavor to a piece of writing, especially travel writing or creative writing. There are also other tools to add flavor to English communication.

Fourth, ice creams are available in ever-growing varieties within a country. Australian Melon, Kabul Pomegranate, Rose Almond, Brazilian Banana, Biscotinno, Malaga, Rum-and-Raisin, Dolcelatte, Wild Berry, Ferror Rocher, French Vanilla, Dry Fruit Falooda, and Belgian Chocolate are all some of the growing varieties of ice creams available in the city of Chennai, India. In addition, ice creams vary across the world. Pistachio Gelato is Italian in origin, Ais Kacang is unique to Malaysia, and Kulfi is an Indian ice cream. English language too has many varieties within a country (for example, in the United States, Texas dialect, New York dialect) or across the world (e.g. American English, British English, Australian English, Canadian English, Indian English). English also varies according to their use in a particular field (e.g. Scientific English, legal English, Creative English, and Screenplay English).

Fifth, if you try to eat an ice cream in one gulp, pain in your facial nerves (technically called "brain freeze" or "ice cream headache") is evident, and you spit all the ice cream.

You would hate not only that ice cream but also the time you would spend on it. But, if you lick it ONE STEP AT A TIME, you would easily swallow it and not spit it. You would enjoy not only the taste but also the time you would spend on it. Because you enjoy the ice cream, the whole experience of ice cream eating will be memorable. Similarly, if you try to learn all the grammar by cramming all the information into your brain, you will experience "brain drain", and you hate English learning. On the other hand, if you take grammar one aspect at a time, and put them into your brain, the whole experience of grammar learning will be easy, enjoyable and, most of all, MEMORABLE—not MEMORIZABLE. This is exactly opposite to taking tests because once the test is over, you will forget everything.

Finally, Eating ice creams will make you thirsty. Salt is one of the main ingredients in ice creams. When you eat ice creams, your blood becomes concentrated with salt, sugar, and other amino acids, which gives the "thirsty" signal to the brain and the body. This thirst is attributed to osmosis. Similarly, learning English and using it for communication will make you thirst for more English knowledge. You automatically learn more English because of ATTRACTION and not out of COMPULSION.

English is not complicated; it is the users of English, especially the teachers, make it complicated. Please understand that I'm not in any way condemning the English teachers. The whole idea of writing this book is to help them realize that there is a simple way to teach English. English teachers have been taught grammar in a complicated way. So they can give only what they have . . . COMPLICATION. The time has come that the old, boring way of English

learning has to change. So if I could convince you, through this book, that there is an easy way—the simple way—to learn English, I would have succeeded in my goal. The magical formula for learning English the ice cream way is this: **9426GM**—that is **9 words, 4 phrases, 2 clauses, 6 sentence types; a few grammar rules; a few mix 'n' match.**

When used simply, English is simple.
—Robert Day, English professor
and Science Editor

This book is not just about what I, as an author, can do to make English learning interesting. It is equally about what you—as a Minister of Education, a school or college administrator, a teacher, a parent, or a student—can do in your own sphere of influence.

If you are a student, you can use this book and learn English in a new way, at your own relaxed time schedule and according to your desire to learn. Above all, you need not have to pass a test. (You may have to get help from other sources to learn complete grammar, because only a few grammar is given in this book.)

If you are a parent, you can read and understand the book, and help your children or other children learn English in a new way.

If you are a teacher, you can use the ice cream method, and help your students learn English quicker and better.

If you are a school or a college administrator, you can implement this new method of learning in your schools or colleges.

If you are a Government leader, especially if you are related to the Ministry of Education, and you get to know the book, you can implement policies to learn English this new way after testing this method in your country. I hope that learning English using this method will transform the lives of the children of your country. Such transformation will change the economy of your nation. English need to be taught as a "life skill" not as a separate language. In addition to implementing good policies, you, as a minister, may also encourage more and more young people to move toward Entrepreneurship. Purpose-based English learning (e.g. Business English) will greatly help them in becoming global business tycoons. So help your citizens learn English, and help your country develop intellectually and economically.

All the best. Keep reading!

> The main hope of a nation lies in the proper education of its youth.
>
> —Erasmus

> We cannot get to the economics without getting to the education.
>
> —Rev. Floyd Fake, Former U.S. Congressman

> Young people are the drivers of economic development. Foregoing this potential is an economic waste and can undermine social stability. It is important to focus on comprehensive and integrated strategies that combine education and trained policies with targeted employment policies for youth.
>
> —Juan Somavia, Director-General of International Labor Organization

ACKNOWLEDGMENTS

To my God and loving savior, Jesus Christ, who exhibited His great love on the cross, and showed me that I'm valuable to Him. (After all, who will die for somebody who is worthless?)

To my wife and my sparkle of life, Hepziba Sigworth, and my son and my treasure in life, Jason Gabriel Sigworth, for their kind cooperation in writing the book.

To my great academic teachers: Dr. K.G. Sivaramakrishnan, Retd. lecturer of Entomology, Madura College, Madurai, for his unceasing advice on developing English skills; Dr. Selvaraja Pandian, Head of the PG Dept. of Zoology and lecturer of Entomology, the American College, Madurai, for his inspiring teaching and for bringing out the information-gathering skills in me.

To Lisa, my Piano teacher residing at San Diego, California, USA, who simplified piano playing and runs the website www.freepianolesssons.com. Her simplification of piano lessons is one of the major inspirations for this book.

To all the spiritual leaders who transformed me through their written and spoken words: Derek Prince, Kenneth Hagin, Joyce Meyer, John Osteen, Joel Osteen, John Hagee, Marilyn Hickey, Morris Cerullo, Jack Hayford, Pat Robertson, Jentezen Franklin, Cindy Jacobs, Francis Frangipane, and Mike Ofoegbu (the author of "dangerous prayer").

To the great gospel Musicians and Worship leaders for their soul-stirring songs, and for their tremendous "Song Writing" skills: Andy Park; Don Moen; Bob Fitts; Brain Doerksen (Canadian singer); Cindy Cruse Ratcliff, Darlene Zschech (Hill Songs, Australia); Graham Kendrick (British singer); John Wimber; Israel Houghton; Lenny Le Blanc; Paul Baloche; Paul Wilbur; Ron Kenoly; Sonic Flood; Steven Curtis Chapman; Twila Paris; and Karen Lim (Singaporean singer).

To all at HOLLYWOOD, for bringing great ideas to screens. I have benefitted a lot from Hollywood for English education, for entertainment, and for enlightenment.

To the founders of "the Hindu" (the Indian English daily), for providing a fabulous newspaper, which is a very good English-learning tool.

To all who are involved in the making of the following published works: New York Public Library manual, American Chemical Society manual, American Medical Association manual, Council of Biological Editors manual, American Psychological Association manual, and Penguin guide to punctuation. Some of the best written-communication ideas are immortalized in these works.

To Dr. A. Venkataraman, the present director of the Copyediting Department, S4 Carlisle Publishing, Chennai for introducing me to the Copyediting world.

To all the authors whose printed work has made me of who I am: Alan Lakein, Ben Sweetland, Beverly LaHaye, Brad Sugars, Brain Tracy, Brendon Burchard, Burke Hedges, Dale Carnegie, Donald Trump, Douglas Andrew, Dr. James

Dobson, Gerry Robert, Graham King, Harv Eker, Harvey Mackay, James Allen, Jim Collins, Joe Vitale, John Adair, Joseph Bailey, Ken Blanchard, Kim Kiyosaki, Mark Victor Hansen, Machen MacDonald, Mike Summey, Morten Hansen, Napoleon Hill, Norman Vincent Peale, Richard Carlson, Robert Kiyosaki, Robert Schuller, Roger Dawson, Roger Hamilton, Russ Whitney, Sean Covey, Sheila Elliott, Stephen Cherniske, Stephen Covey, Steve Gottry, and Tim LaHaye.

To Farrina Gailey and Nelson Cortez (publishing consultants at Partridge) for picking me as an author and shooking me with the idea of writing a book for the global audience.

To all at Partridge who made this book a reality.

To the Founders of the good book stores of Chennai—Landmark, Higginbothams, and Starmark—for making available fabulous books to the general public. Had I not purchased some good books there, this book would have not been written.

To Dr. Karunanidhi, the Former Chief Minister of Tamil Nadu, for his initiative in setting up Anna Centenary Library, the state-of-the-art library in Chennai.

To all the staff at Anna Centenary Library for helping me access the resources.

To all the staffs at Connemara Library, Chennai for helping me access the resources. I appreciate their good attitude toward the library users and toward the upkeep of the library.

To my former colleagues at Techset Composition India (a subsidiary of Techset Composition, London) for their advice or support in this project: Tamil Selvam, Senior Copyeditor, for his help in accessing the right resources in the library; Mrs. Saraswathi Prabakaran, Senior English-Language editor, for her inputs on barriers to English learning; Alfred George, Senior English-Language editor, for his insights on writing to the Ministers of Education.

Last but highly emphatic, to the founders of British Council, for making available great resources in English learning, and for all the friendly staff at British Council (especially Preethi Padmanaban, Maria Jeromi, Anita, and John), helping me access the resources.

FOR WHOM THIS BOOK IS WRITTEN?

When a speaker won't boil it down, the audience must sweat it out.

—Unknown

When the authors won't make it clear "whom the book is for", the right audience may miss the book. In written and spoken communication, the foremost goal of a writer or speaker is: TO FIND THE AUDIENCE. This book is written in a broader perspective and opens the minds of the students to a plethora of possibilities they can realize by mastering English communication. I took a significant amount of time pondering and reflecting on who are the people who can benefit from this book. The result is this section.

When people communicate, they focus too much on the features of the product or service instead of answering the question, "Can you help me?" The key is to focus on benefits, not features.

—Jerry Weissman, *Presenting to Win*

In general, this book's target audience is: Every teacher (especially, school or college administrators), every parent, every student, and every professional using English as a medium of communication. Students and teachers being the major beneficiaries, I will specify the target audience for this book as clearly as possible. The people who find the book most useful include:

- Students preparing for various civil service examinations
- Students preparing for IELTS, TOEFL, SAT, GRE, GMAT, MCAT, LSAT, USMLE, CPA examinations
- Students leaving their homeland to English-speaking countries to pursue their higher studies
- Students who need to submit writing assignments or their academic dissertation
- Anyone want to know the Job prospects in English language
- Research scholars already enrolled or about to enroll in a PhD program
- Scientists interested in improving their technical communication, especially written communication
- All English teachers and private English-coaching tutors
- People aspiring for jobs in Publishing houses, advertising, journalism, and media
- All budding copyeditors and writers
- Aspirants or existing professionals willing to improve their English communication
- All parents who don't want to leave the responsibility of teaching English language to their children into someone else's hands, and all who want to give their children an early start in Standard English

Readers please understand that this is not a watered-down English grammar book. It is a neatly packed and simplified form of Standard English, which is only known to and appreciated by professionals, but is very well needed for every communicator who uses English. If you are a person just wanting to clear the exam and forget grammar for the rest of your life, this book is not for you. Equally, this book is not for pleasure reading, even though at least about one-third of the book is written to give you enough reading pleasure. This is an action-engaging book.

This book needs to be consulted to as long as you master English communication, especially written communication. Both the author and the publisher have taken enough care in bringing out the book as readable and portable as possible. The book is designed to be small because you will feel it light and easy to carry. The book has enough inspirations for every expected and unexpected reader. I hope that, upon reading this book, the readers will no longer DREAD GRAMMAR but TREAD GRAMMAR, and become excellent communicators.

HOW TO READ THIS BOOK?

Some books are to be tasted ... others to be swallowed ... and more few to be chewed and digested.
—Francis Bacon

Generally, when you purchase any electronic device, you will be given a users' manual to help you use the device to your advantage. Keeping this thought in mind, I added this section to help the readers take advantage of the several pieces of information given in this book.

The book is divided into three parts for easy reading and understanding. Because this book has a lot of interesting examples to capture your attention, and is based on "Ice cream" theme, I can say that this book is to be tasted. However, there are parts to be swallowed (Part II) and parts to be chewed and digested (Part III and IV).

Part I gives you the background information on English— The history of English language, its development, the varieties of English, American English and its dialects, barriers to learn English, what is the best way to learn English, benefits of learning English, and Job prospects in various Industries—Medical transcription, Call Centre, Medical Billing, Mass Media, HOLLYWOOD, Animation, Publishing, Music Industry, Tourism, Science, Teaching, Aviation, Hospitality, Business, and Law.

Part II constitutes the existing methods of English learning",
the best way to learn English, and the ice cream way to learn
English.

Part III is the core of the book—Grammar and its role;
words, phrases, clauses, sentences, paragraphs; and various
punctuation marks and their roles. Part III being the tough
meat, you need to take time to eat (grasp) and digest (retain)
the book. In this book, the grammar concepts have been
flagged as "Ice cream 1", "Ice cream 2", "Ice cream 3", etc.
Some ice creams are short, some are big, and some may be
extra large. So some "ice creams" have been divided into
many licks—"lick 1", "lick 2", "lick 3", etc. So don't rush
through grammar. Have only one ice cream a day and have
only one lick per day; the other licks of the same ice cream
can be had during the upcoming days (see Study Plan in
Appendix II). The way of dividing grammar into" ice creams
and licks" helps you to divide your learning. Remember:
sorting helps in mastering.

While taking only one grammar aspect per day, you can add
any relevant information from other books to aid in your
learning. Alternatively, you can learn the entire grammar
given in the book, and later on supplement the learning
using other books. It is not learning more information is
important. Your learning must be transferrable in your
day-to-day communication—either written or spoken, or
both. If your learning is not helping for practical living, it is
of no use to learn more.

> Doing more of what doesn't work won't make it work
> any better.
>
> —Charles J. Givens

You can read this book in several ways. You can read the entire book from cover to cover. You can straight away go to the individual chapters that are appealing to you the most. If you feel like reading the book later, but just want to flip through the pages to see if there is anything interesting, you can read the quotations, look through the pictures, or read just one chapter, especially chapter 6: Learn English the ice cream way.

So, go ahead. Mark up your book. Use a pen, a pencil, colored pencils, a highlighter, or different highlighters. Maybe, you can use a pink highlighter for information on other books. Similarly, you can use green highlighter for marking quotations, yellow for important points, and orange for any illustration or examples. You may also use some symbols or some kind of markings. You may also opt for writing in the margins or write it on "post-it notes" and stick it in your book. If you use the book this way, you will make the book very much personal for you. That is, you will understand the message in this book better, and you may easily come back to the book and spot any particular area for future reference.

PART I

BACKGROUND

CHAPTER 1

Introduction

If you can measure it, you can make it.

—Napoleon Hill

Sorting and Keeping

Imagine your childhood time in which you watched your mum washing clothes and keep them ready for later use. Your mum would be surrounded by loads of dried clothes—clothes of your mum, those of your dad, those of you, and those of your siblings—and she has the daunting task of organizing it in a wardrobe. As a small child, you may have wondered about two things:

1. How would she fit this massive amount of clothes into one wardrobe?

2. How long would it take for mum to do all these chores?

As you watch, all that your mum does is SORTING and KEEPING similar items as one group, ONE STEP AT A TIME.

After a certain time, this massive load of clothes would vanish from the scene, and you could see steeples of clothes categorized and neatly organized. Finally, all the clothes would easily fit into the wardrobe. You could have seen this a million times, but not with this awareness. Not only this time-consuming task will be completed, but it is done in a step-by-step and enjoyable way. You may say, how this boring task is enjoyable? Well, your mother might have been singing all the way and not focusing on the time but on each moment—ONE TASK AT A TIME.

Much the same way, you, as a child, wondered about doing the laundry, anyone who wants to learn English would have two basic questions in their minds:

1. How am I going to learn all the vocabulary, all the grammar and other concepts, and put it into my brain?

2. How much time it takes to learn the language?

Generally, all learners get caught up with the complexity of English.

If I could tell you that there is an easy, enjoyable, and memorable way to learn English—the simple English not the complex English—won't you not get stirred up? Well, read further.

English language has two components: *vocabulary* and *grammar*. Even though English has a massive vocabulary of more than half a million words, and the English professors have made numerous rules (grammar), you can still learn English the easy way. You may ask how? I would say by *sorting* and *keeping*.

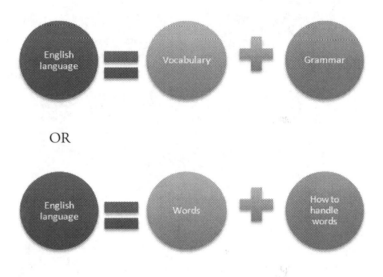

OR

Mystery or Mastery?

Why we need to sort or classify things? If we classify things, we can easily measure them. If we can measure them, we can manage them. If we can manage them, we can master them.

Librarians at public libraries sort and keep thousands and thousands of books because we all can locate and use books with ease. If they fail to do so, all we can see is a room with a heap of books, messing the beauty of the available space. The same is the case with someone who learns only vocabulary and not grammar. His/her writing will only be a heap of words, messing the beauty of communication.

> Without yardstick there is no measurement. And without measurement there is no control [managing].
> —Pravin M. Shah, Indian Management

While happen to see a piano, many would look at it, fiddle with the keys, and make some noise. Piano is a MYSTERY for them. When a concert pianist happens to see a new piece of piano at a music store, that pianist too would fiddle with the keys, but bring forth sounds that captivate those nearby. Piano is MASTERY for that player. The difference is practice. The noise makers seldom work with the piano, but concert pianists sit for hours and hours to learn the various aspects that would help them to have mastery over the piano.

Many know that piano playing is a complex art—you need to understand the symbols, the notations, how to read music sheets, how to play with both hands, and you need to overcome what is called "hand freeze". This is similar to the "brain freeze" that hasty ice cream eaters would encounter. Thank God for my Piano teacher! She simplified piano playing. Otherwise, I would have hated piano learning.

It is so awkward at their initial time of learning that though the players know how to play, but somehow their hands won't cooperate but would stay frozen. But this obstacle lasts only for a time—maybe some week's time. If the players persist and patiently keep playing and keep practicing that hurdle would be crossed. Soon the players' hands would glide over the keys, and waves and waves of sweet music would soothe the ears and the minds of the listeners. Such rigorous practice would pay them back and they can become millionaires if they can reach the masses via their music production. Grammar is needed even for music production because songwriting requires English words, and English words require grammar for their proper use.

Someone said that Beethoven and Mozart didn't wait for some inspiration to make great composing. They regularly practice; sometimes it could have made them feel bored. Also, they need to overlook the loneliness, not getting the notes correct, etc. They need to overcome these barriers before reaping the rewards of their practice. We all know the mesmerizing composing these two great legends have blessed us with.

> You cannot play symphonies until you have mastered the notes.
>
> —Dr. Edward L. Kramer

> The great composer does not set to work because he is inspired, but becomes inspired because he is working. Beethoven, Wagner, Bach, and Mozart settled down day after day to the job in hand. They didn't waste time waiting for inspiration.
>
> —Ernest Newman

Initially, grammar may appear dry and boring. Once you have a purpose and you persist in your learning, you won't have to think of grammar again in your life. Whenever you use English, you need grammar. But, if you achieve some mastery, you won't think of grammar consciously. Good grammar becomes natural and automatic to you.

Whether English is a mystery or mastery depends on how much time you took to get to know it, or on how intelligently you learnt it. You need time to get to know a person before you develop deep friendship with that person. If a dictionary is given to a lay person, he or she will flip some pages and leave it back soon. Dictionary is a mystery to a lay person. If you give the same dictionary to an editor or a writer, you will see the emergence of polished writing. Using a dictionary is mastery for an editor or a writer.

Simplifying Complex English via Sorting

All the English words (approximately more than 5,00,000 words) can be SORTED into 9 words, and you can easily learn a few simple rules and keep it in your mind. Then you can mix words to form phrases and clauses. There are only 4 main types of phrases and 2 types of clauses. Using phrases and clauses, you can create your own sentences—the basic units of thoughts. You may ask: how many types of sentences are there in English? Only 6 types. Now, you can group sentences to construct paragraphs—the basic units of written or spoken communication. See how the big globe of "complex English" is now turned into a small globe of "simple English":

Remember my magical formula: **9426GM—9 words, 4 phrases, 2 clauses, 6 sentence types; a few grammar rules; some mix 'n' match** (mixing words to form phrases; mixing phrases and clauses to form sentences; mixing sentences to form paragraphs). That's all! Is this not good news? You can easily remember my formula (see the following illustration) by fixing it in your mind as "9426 Gentle Men".

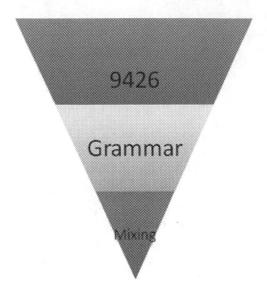

Men are interested in getting a match (dating beautiful women) by showing their gentleness. You can get a match of words by applying grammar.

Using vocabulary and grammar, you can build words. Taking words, grammar, syntax, and punctuation, you change words to sentences. Using logic and length concepts of sentences, and punctuation you can build paragraphs. Using many logically arranged paragraphs, you can communicate—via writing or speaking.

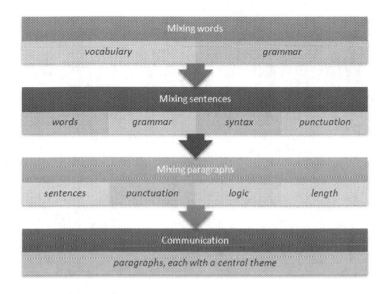

Just like a magician bringing out rabbits, kerchiefs, and doves from an empty hat, out of a mind comes essays, poems, and stories. If somebody asks you how, now you will easily answer **9426GM**. Yes! **9 words, 4 phrases, 2 clauses, 6 sentences, some grammar, some mixing.**

> Man's word is his magic wand filled with magic and power!
>
> —Florence Scovel Shinn

Like your mum, now you too can sing your way through this daunting and boring task—English learning—and not DREAD grammar but TREAD grammar! I will show you how to do that in the rest of the chapters.

CHAPTER 2

Where Does English Come From? How it Developed?

Language is the blood of the soul into which thoughts run and out of which they grow.

—Oliver Wendell Holmes

The Origin of English Language

If you pick a common English word, and see how it is written in other languages, you can find a same pattern across different languages, as shown in the following illustration.

English	French	German	Spanish	Italian
•South	•Sud	•Süden	•Sud	•Sud

This can lead us to the logic that these languages might have evolved from one common root. This is similar to the idea that all the different races of humans might have originated from one common ancestor—Adam and Eve, the first man and woman.

Just like we all have a common ancestry, English too has a family tree. English evolved from the root of an original language called Proto-Indo-European. Even though there is no accurate record of its beginning, it is known that it was being spoken in Eastern Europe at least six thousand years ago.

The people who used Proto-Indo-European language were originally gypsies. As time progressed, they slowly become different tribes and moved all over Europe, and settled in as far as India. The geographical spread of the tribes initiated a change in their language to a great extent. As a result, each tribe developed its own dialect of Proto-Indo-European. Quickly, those dialects developed into distinct languages.

Similarly, English has developed into distinct varieties in many Anglophone countries (US, UK, Canada, Australia, and New Zealand) or in countries where English is the second or official language (e.g., India). Now let us see how English is developed in its country of Origin, England.

> The language [English] is perpetually in flux: it is a living stream, shifting, changing, receiving new strength from thousand tributaries, losing old forms in the backwaters of time.
> —William Strunk Jr. & E.B. White, *Elements of Style*.

Old English (450-1100 A.D.)

History of Old English

The early speakers of English comprise two tribes called Angles and Saxons. Attracted by its fertility, the Angles and Saxons migrated to the island of Britain, around 450 A.D. A Celtic tribe already inhabited the island, and they are known as the Britons. In those times, it is perfectly legal to acquire new territories by waging war against the original inhabitants. So the Anglo-Saxons attacked and killed the Britons and settle down in that new land called "land of

13

Angles" or Englalond, which was later known as "England". (Note: Germany is called in their native language as Deutschland, i.e. Deutsch + land. The land of Thai people is called Thailand. Using this logic, you can easily derive England = English + land, i.e. the land of English.) At that time, the language of the Anglo-Saxons is known as "Old English".

Old English is similar to Modern English in several ways. The Anglo-Saxons used many of the same words we use today, in a slightly different form:

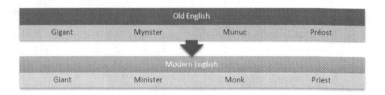

Old English			
Gigant	Mynster	Munuc	Préost

Modern English			
Giant	Minister	Monk	Priest

Although there are some similarities, Old English differed from Modern English in terms of structure. Modern English uses word order (syntax) to show the role of each word in a sentence, whereas Old English used many different word endings to indicate gender, number, case, and person. For example, the old English word "hund" (the modern English equivalent of this "hund" is "hound") had to be written as *hund, hundes, hunde, hundas, hunda* or *hundum,* according to its use in a sentence.

Development of Old English

By around 600 A.D., Christian missionaries went about converting the English people to Christianity. Those missionaries introduced a new language as well as a new religion. Learning Latin, the language of the church, had been a main activity for many educated English people. Soon, Latin got its way into English language, as the English people borrowed many Latin words and made them part of their language. *School*, *altar*, *candle*, and *paper* are all words borrowed from Latin.

Later, the English people also borrowed new words from another set of people called Vikings. By around 790, Vikings from Scandinavia began to attack Britain and established their rule for the next several centuries. As a result, many Vikings had to settle in England. This gave way to the entry of Old Norse into Old English. Many of the words beginning with "sc" or "sk" are from Old Norse.

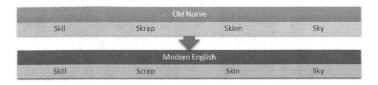

Middle English (1100-1500)

In 1066, England was attacked again, but by a different people—the Normans from France. William of Normandy led a historic battle against the English people. The victory of French at this battle—the Battle of Hastings—changed the course of English. That fateful French victory brought the English people under French rule for the next 150 years. French became the language of government, law, business, and literature; however, Latin remained the language of religion. The English people who received schooling were educated in these two languages. Just like the Church language and Viking's language got into the main stream English, French too contributed to the rich vocabulary of English. English words linked to power and wealth were borrowed from French, after the Norman Conquest:

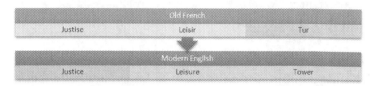

Old French		
Justise	Leisir	Tur

Modern English		
Justice	Leisure	Tower

A feast of animal flesh and a feast of loan words

Some of the common words we use give a clue to how life was in England after the Norman Conquest. The English peasants tend the livestock, whereas the French nobles chose to "feast" (which is again a French word) on the meats. So it is no wonder that words related to livestock such as *hog*, *calf,* and *sheep* came to us from Old English, but words representing animal flesh such as *bacon*, *veal,* and *mutton* were borrowed from Old French.

French, the language of the educated at that time, was used for almost all written communication. But English didn't die. It was still the language spoken by the common people—the farmers, herdsmen, servants, and craftsmen. As these people continue to speak English, the language changed from Old English into a better form of English—the Middle English. This change was brought forth by "grammar". For example, the Old English word "hund" had six different forms, but the speakers of Middle English kept only two forms—"hund" and "hundes".

The triumph of English language

Even though there was a possibility of French becoming the national language of England, English language ultimately triumphed. This could be attributed to two things: (i) The English people outnumbered the French rulers; (ii) The Normans in England gradually lost contact with France. In the Mid-1300s, educated people of England were again using English for writing as well as for speaking.

Modern English (1500-Present)

Several different things happened to English as the language entered a modern era. Pronunciation, grammar, and spelling were standardized, and English expanded into an international language. This modern era of English language is marked by three things: the Great Vowel Shift, the London dialect setting the standard of the modern language, and the English people's quest for riches in foreign lands.

The Great Vowel Shift

The sounds of the Middle English are very different from the present day English. According to historians, in 14th century, the word "care" sounded like "car", "meek" was pronounced as "make", and "bite" sounded like "beet". There were gradual changes in pronunciation. By the late 14th century, pronunciation was completely revised for betterment. This shift in pronunciation is called the Great Vowel Shift.

London Dialect becoming the standard of Modern English

By 1500 A.D., almost everyone in England spoke English. However, there is no established standard for the language for a long time; different regions of England used different dialects. The Scribes of England wrote English in their own dialect and spelled words according to the way they chose. However, the dialect of London got pre-eminence because London became the centre of English culture, business, and trade.

The setting up of the first Printing press in England by William Caxton in the year 1476 requires a special mention here. He began printing books in London dialect, and printed books soon spread like a wild fire across England. More and more people were buying books because of its low cost and easy replication of information than conventional hand-copied scripts. This gave forth to the need for fixing the spellings of many words in print, and soon London dialect became a national standard.

Followingly, books on correct English usage, spelling, and pronunciation appeared on the market. People began compiling extensive lists of "hard words" and their definitions. This gave birth to the compilation of exhaustive words in sequence called dictionaries. Even though English has become standardized, it never stopped changing. When the first printing shop was opened, the Renaissance was sweeping England, igniting a renewed interest in the classical languages. This resulted in the entry of Greek and Latin words into English, enriching the English vocabulary still more.

English people's quest for riches in foreign lands

In 16th century, English people began to travel abroad to seek out wealth in foreign lands, using sea routes. As they discovered new places, they started trading and colonizing those countries, eventually establishing their rule.

Historians recorded that the first New World settlement was established in Jamestown in 1607. British and French began to fight to claim this new land called Canada. Eventually, British won the war, and Canada was under British rule in 1763. Followingly, in the 17th century, West Indian islands of Antigua, Barbados, Jamaica, St Kitts, and Trinidad and Tobago all were brought under British rule.

Captain Cook's voyages between 1768 and 1779 led to the discovery of Australia and New Zealand. At that time, Dutch was overthrown in South Africa, as the British took control. In the latter part of the century, there was a fierce competition from Britain, Belgium, France, Germany, and Portugal to establish their rule in the remaining parts of Africa. Finally, British claimed Nigeria, Kenya and Tanzania, and Zimbabwe, which represent West, East, and Southern Africa, respectively. India was brought under British rule in 1750.

It seems like the Anglo-Saxons' spirit of acquiring new lands continued even long after their initial conquest over Britons. In their early invasion, they killed the inhabitants to acquire a new land. Since the times have changed, the English people changed their approach to trading and colonizing, instead of invading and killing. This ultimately gave way to English becoming an international language. This also led to the borrowing of new words from other languages. A few examples are given below.

The Rise of American English

When English people colonized the Western Hemisphere, they borrowed words from Native American languages, invented new words, and changed the pronunciations and uses of some old words. In addition, they kept some old words and old pronunciations, and the grammatical uses that the British support in England began to change. By 1776, the American dialect grew so much that it was called American English.

Native Americans, Africans who came as slaves, and immigrants from other countries all have left their mark on American English. The following are the loan words from several other countries:

As America has emerged as a world power, American English has soon become the standard for English in the 20th century. And, American English has spread to the remote parts of the globe via American television, radio, movies, books, and newspapers.

Regional dialects of American English

If you happen to listen to a person from Texas and to a person from New York or to someone from Massachusetts, you can find that there are differences in their language. It is said that Americans use three different regional dialects: Northern, Midland, and Southern. To make it simple, these dialects include differences in terms of pronunciation or vocabulary, and sometimes grammar.

It has been said that 'barn' is pronounced as 'bahn' in some parts of the United States. People of midland and southern United States tend to add an 'r' sound to the words. For example, 'wash' is pronounced as 'warsh'.

It is generally known that soft drinks are called *tonic* in Boston, but in other parts of the United States, it is called *soda* or *pop*. People of Southern United States say "sick **at** my stomach", whereas individuals from North say "sick **to** my stomach". Note the prepositional difference in both speeches.

Global English

What just started as a dialect spoken by just a few Anglo-Saxons has now become the most widely used language in the world. It is said that more than about one-third of the whole world speak English. In 1990, English became an official language in 87 countries. The growth of information technology has made English more and more universal, as most of the software documentation is made in English, and duplicating it in other languages is costly, time-consuming, and sometimes forbidden. Now English has become the world language of commerce, science, teaching, computers, and air-traffic control.

CHAPTER 3

Barriers to English Learning

When I see a barrier, I cry and I curse, and then I get a ladder and climb over it.

—John Johnson

People's perception of barriers to English learning

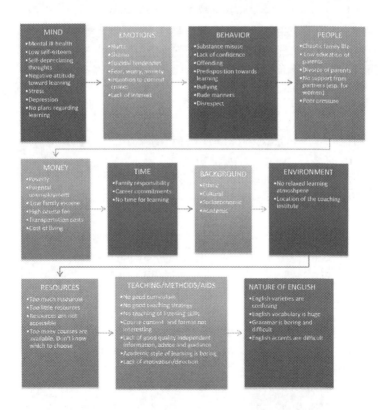

When I thought of writing about the barriers to English learning, I searched in Google. I read the articles of people from different parts of the world. When I read those articles, I understand that people have a lot to say about what they consider as barriers to English learning. I have summarized them in the above illustration for your easy reference.

This illustration contains quite a lot of things that people are struggling with. Well, this book may answer some of the problems mentioned under resources, teaching, and nature of English. You need to take action to cross the barriers in the rest of the categories, but I will try to address these in a short form in the upcoming paragraphs. Those categories of barriers can be handled if you develop a strong, healthy mind. Please take a look at the following quotes that will show the importance of the power of mind:

Mind's connection with mental illness, poverty, and crime

Mental health expert Sherri Wittwer says: "There is no shame in having a mental illness. Mental illness is no different than any other illness such as asthma or diabetes. What we do know is that treatment works, recovery is possible, and there is hope." Poverty and crime has a strong connection with self-hatred, another condition of the mind:

Self-hate is a form of mental slavery that results in poverty, ignorance, and crime.

—Susan L. Taylor

> There is a way to provide against the onslaught of poverty. It is the recognition of the power of mind.
>
> —A.G. Gaston

> Poverty is a degrading, dehumanizing, cancer-like disease of the uninformed mind.
>
> —Mark Victor Hansen

Mind's connection with faith and belief

Napoleon Hill, Joseph Edward, and Og Mandio show us the importance of the mind's connection with faith and unbelief:

> You can be anything you want to be, if only you believe with sufficient conviction and act in accordance with your faith; for whatever the mind can conceive and believe, the mind can achieve.
>
> —Napoleon Hill

> The law of Attraction attracts to you everything you need, according to the nature of your thought of life. Your environment and financial condition are the perfect reflection of your habitual thinking.
>
> —Joseph Edward

> Always have faith that conditions will change. Though your heart be heavy and your body bruised and your purse empty, and there is no one to comfort you—hold on. Just as you know the sun will rise, so also believe that your period of misfortune must end. It was always so. It will always be.
>
> —Og Mandino

Mind's connection with our destiny, our joys, and our ills

The following are the proof to the mind's involvement in our destiny, joy and ills:

You become what you consciously think about.

—Earl Nightingale

Mind is the master power that moulds and makes and man is mind. And ever more he takes the tool of thought and shaping what he wills, brings forth a thousand joys, a thousand ills. He thinks in secret and it comes to pass. Environment is but a looking glass.

—James Allen

The world we have created is a product of our thinking; it cannot be changed without changing our thinking.

—Albert Einstein

You not only create your life with your thoughts, but your thoughts add powerfully to the creation of the world. If you thought that you were insignificant and had no power in this world, think again. Your mind is actually shaping the world around you.

—Rhonda Byrne

Mind's connection with money or financial problems

Financial or money problems have their share in the realm of mind, as shown below:

> It is impossible to solve your financial problems with money.
>
> —Phil Laut

> Money will only give your financial problems temporary relief.
>
> —Bob Proctor

> Wealth is largely a result of habit.
>
> —Jack Astor

> It's true we don't have much money so what we have to do is THINK.
>
> —Prof. Ernest Rutherford [*Emphasis added*]

> Empty pockets never held anyone back. Only empty heads and empty hearts can do that.
>
> —Norman Vincent Peale

Mind's connection with your living conditions

See the following quotes to realize how the mind affects one's living conditions:

> The mind in itself, in its own place, can make a hell out of heaven and heaven out of hell.
>
> —John Milton

People are anxious to improve their circumstances, but unwilling to improve themselves, they therefore remain bound.

—James Allen

The greatest discovery of my generation is that human beings can alter their lives by altering their attitudes of mind.

—William James

Minds connection with your beauty

Finally, the mind has its say in our beauty:

Wouldn't it be interesting if what was on the inside of a person were revealed on the outside? Then we would know who the truly beautiful people of the world are.

—Neal Maxwell

People are like stained-glass windows. They sparkle and shine when the sun is out, but when the darkness sets in their true beauty is revealed only if there is light from within.

—Elisabeth kübler-Ross

The Author's perception of English-learning barriers

Having addressed what the majority of people perceived as barriers, now I focus on what I perceive to be the barriers to English learning. Some of my perception of English-learning barriers may match those expressed by the majority. Basically, there are three types of barriers to learn English: self-imposed, Environmental, and methodical.

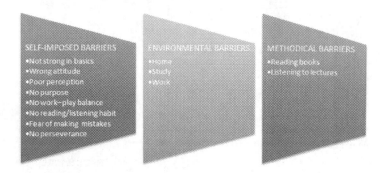

SELF-IMPOSED BARRIERS

(i) Not strong in English Basics

The primary barrier is *not having a firm foundation of English learning* (basically grammar). Some may appear to speak good English, but could not understand the difference between subject-verb agreement and subjunctive mood. When they come across sentences such as "If I were you . . .", they would say "If I was you" is the correct form, convincing others that they are following the subject-verb agreement. Not realizing that "If I were you . . ." is a part of grammar called subjunctive mood. They are like a plant whose roots are not firm in the ground. Any time they may collapse when the storm of test hits them.

Wide view   Close view

To bring this point come alive to the readers, I have added a plant photograph that I recently captured in my garden (see illustration above). This photograph is very significant for me because while writing this book Nature gave me a powerful illustration to support this point. Can you see that, the main root (the tap root) is out of soil, but the secondary roots have gone deeper into the soil? If not for the secondary roots, the plant would have already died. Maybe the plant struggled to survive and put some secondary roots into the soil to sustain itself momentarily. Unless a caring gardener puts the main root into the soil, the chances of plant survival are very low. (Teachers, you are the caring gardener to tenderly handle the main root of students' potential and put it inside the soil.) In much the same way, when we say we know English and could not communicate properly, we too cannot sustain in this World. We may manage to get our secondary roots into the soil and appear nice, but when tough circumstances come our way, we would only be embarrassed.

A house, along with its foundation, is only as stable as the ground upon which it rests.

—Unknown

(ii) Wrong attitude

Education is more to do with your attitude. If you have a positive mental attitude toward learning, you will learn very well. If you have a negative or loser's attitude, you will never learn anything. A student should have a child-like attitude toward learning. No child in this world ever get tired of repeatedly falling down on their way to learning to walk. They never stop trying to stand irrespective of how many times they fall.

> Nothing can stop the man with the right mental attitude from achieving his goal; nothing on earth can help the man with the wrong mental attitude.
>
> —W.W. Ziege

> Birds make great sky circles of their freedom. How do they learn it? They fall, and by falling, they are given wings.
>
> —Rumi, Sufi Poet

> Success is going from failure to failure without losing enthusiasm.
>
> —Winston Churchill

Probably, the no. 1 learning barrier among people who know some English is the predisposition that "I know English". If a person is not practicing English, the chances are that he or she still needs to know English. Take, for example, a graduate who studied in English medium or English-only instruction all of his life. When encouraged to speak or write, he or she may do an amateur way of speaking or writing but he or she can't do public speaking or write Standard English unless practicing those arts.

Why do so many "English-knowers" go for IELTS, TOEFL, GMAT, GRE coaching classes before appearing for their respective English-testing examinations. If they are "English-knowers", why they need to learn English again? Because the English they know is not sufficient enough to graduate from those examinations. After completing my IELTS I became proud that I got certified from Cambridge, UK. That's a good pride. But I was too proud that I became an "English-knower". Now, that is a bad pride. When I stepped into the world of copyediting, I realized that how much of English I still need to know, and that English is called Standard English, which is a form of English practiced in all careful writing—academic, scientific, business, and law.

Not only the so-called English-knowers need English education, scientists, research scholars, lawyers, business executives, advertisers, people aspiring to enter Hollywood, or anyone under the sun sure need English education, or rather a special English education (Scientific English, Legal English, Business English, Creative English, or Screenplay English, etc.).

> Knowledge is proud he has learned so much; wisdom is humble he knows no more.
>
> —William Cooper

> The only things worth learning are the things you learn after you know it all.
>
> —Harry Truman

(iii) Poor perception

We all have our perceptions of other people, general ideas, and life and living. Our perceptions may be right or wrong. They may be rich or poor. You may think that a particular person is a jerk or stupid, smart or rich. Not only we have perceptions of others, we all have perception of ourselves. Your perception about yourself decides your fate or destiny. If you perceive yourself as a scholar, you will eventually become a scholar. If you perceive yourself as a dropout, you will be dropped out from your school or college. Similarly, when a student perceives that he or she can learn English well, it will turn out that that person will eventually learn English well. If you take time to read this book, your perception of English learning will surely change. If you suffer from poor perception, change your perception now. Anybody can learn English, irrespective of whatever barrier they may face.

(iv) No sense of purpose

The fourth barrier is not having *a sense of purpose*. Why someone disappears from the world with nothing accomplished, while few others achieve extraordinary things? The achievers will have a purpose and a passion. If you are a person of purpose, you take action towards achieving that purpose.

> He who has a "why" to live for can bear almost any "how."
>
> —Friedrich Nietzche

If you know the "why", understanding the "how" would be easy. Let us go to the business world for a moment. An aspiring businessman needs to write a business plan, whose first point is drafting the mission statement—why an aspirant needs to be in business? Without the "why", "how" would be meaningless. I wrote this book because I have a strong "why"—to help those who are struggling to learn English. Otherwise, I wouldn't have sacrificed my sleep, my time, and my money to bring my thoughts into print. So if you have the answer to "why you need to study English", you would learn English at all costs.

> It must be borne in mind that the tragedy of life doesn't lie in not reaching your goal. The tragedy lies in having no goal to reach ... Not failure, but low aim is sin.
>
> —Dr. Benjamin E. Bays

(v) No work–play balance

Keeping a balance in every area of our lives would make our living a truly joyful experience. If you work, work, and work, you will have lot of stress. Stress is not good to your body beyond a certain point. Contrarily, if you just play, play, and play, you will not learn the things you need to learn. You will become bored after a certain period of time. So the key is to have a balance between both work and play.

> All work and no play makes Jack a dull boy; but all play and no work makes him something greatly worse.
>
> —Samuel Smiles

While learning English, instead of cramming all the grammar into your brain, it is better to have a study plan and stick to that plan (see Study Plan in Appendix II).

> Ram it in—Jam it in,
> Students' head are hollow.
> Cram it in—Slam it in,
> There is more to follow.
> > —Elmer Towns, Professor and Dean
> > at Liberty University, in his comment about teaching

Your learning would be much better if you take baby steps instead of giant leaps. Giant leaps may be exciting for a while, but you may suddenly have a fall because the rhythm of learning will be lost. In the music world, it is not how fast a song is played that matters. All that matters is how well the rhythm of the song is maintained from beginning to end. English learning is like running a marathon, not a 100 meters race.

> True progress in any field is a relay race and not a single event.
> > —Cavett Roberts

So, if you study only one concept a day, and complement your learning by reading, writing, playing crosswords or word games such as scrabble, or watching a movie, you learning will be exciting. You may even listen to songs and learn English because song composing takes song-writing skills. And, song-writing needs grammar.

(vi) No reading or listening habit

The fifth is the lack of *reading* or *listening* habit. The reading or listening habit alone would be sufficient to attain a decent proficiency in English. But be careful WHAT YOU READ or WHAT YOUR LISTEN. That is, you need to choose the best writers or the best speakers to get good English. If you put in bad English from others, your English will only be bad.

> Resolve to edge in a little reading every day, if it is but a single sentence. If you gain 15 minutes a day, it will make itself felt at the end of the year.
>
> —Horace Mann

> The choice of books, like that of friends, is a serious duty. We are responsible for what we read as what we do.
>
> —John Lubbock

(vii) *Fear of making mistakes*

Mistakes are the way to learn. Mistakes, mistakes and mistakes, and correcting, correcting, correcting is the only way to success. Our education system generally won't allow the students to make mistakes. Take for example, the process of writing a letter or a report. Some teachers cannot stand when there are strike-off markings in students' writing. The students are expected to give a clean write up, a perfect paper with no strike marks. But you ask any Best-selling author, they would strike off their writing several times before perfecting their work for the intended readers. Don't be annoyed about such teachers. Don't be afraid of making mistakes. Do your work, come what may. You can correct the mistakes at any point of time.

> While one person hesitates because he feels inferior, the other is busy making mistakes and becoming superior.
>
> —Henry C. Link

> Mistakes are the portals of discovery.
>
> —James Joyce

> What is a mistake? Nothing but education, nothing but first step to something better.
>
> —Wendell Phillips

(vii) *Lack of perseverance*

We may be enthusiastic about English learning and have a good start, and working our way towards our finish line—good communication. But, we may stuck somewhere in the middle. Maybe our negative circumstances, some setbacks, or any other thing that may disturb us deeply. In such times, we have to remind ourselves our purpose of learning. We have to develop our tenacity muscle and persevere in our goal of English learning. Remember: Perseverance is exactly opposite to complaining.

Writing this book drove me crazy. It almost killed me. I spent so many sleepless nights. Sometimes right ideas won't come. In certain times, I didn't have the right source to look to. Sometimes, I get stuck in a chapter. In those circumstances, negative thoughts began to blow me up. I thought of giving up of writing this book. But I reminded myself that If I don't write, it would not benefit me or my readers. I reminded myself of my purpose—the task of simplifying English learning for the benefit of many. Soon my enthusiasm came back and I persevered in every hardship that came my way—no good sleep, ignoring my family, not talking to my friends enough, suffered severe pain in my forehead and thigh muscles, had back pain, enormous stress, and mindless eating. Finally, the book is written!

> Perseverance and tact are the two most important qualities for the individual who wants to move ahead.
> —Benjamin Disraeli

ENVIRONMENTAL BARRIERS

(viii) Home/study/work environment

Another significant barrier is Environment. All of us know that certain plants grow well in certain geographic areas. For example, certain orchids are reported to grow very well in Singapore because that country has the right environment, the ideal climate: 30°C and 80% humidity.

Which environment you need to be in if you want to improve your intelligence? you may go to a library, a book store, or a school. What are the ideal places for improving your health? you have to go to the gym or to a jogger's park. Similarly, if you want to have a peaceful mind, you need to go to a church, to a meditation centre, or to a Japanese garden. So, if you want to learn English, you have to find a good English-learning environment. The learning environment may be your home, your school/college, or the place where you work. If your home, study, or work environment is not enhancing English learning, you have to find a good environment that supports you in becoming a good English communicator. If you're in need of a good, English-learning environment, I strongly recommend that you join a good English-coaching institute.

Now I illustrate with my own need to find a right environment when I had to use internet. I'm living in a suburb where internet cafés are very minimal. Even if some exist, they are of poor standards. One day I happen to go to an internet café in an adjacent neighborhood. The ambience is nice; the owner is educated, friendly, and accommodative; beyond that, the browsing speed is considerably good. And in that environment, I get quick internet links to finding publishers. And in that environment, I find the publisher of this book, Partridge India. Had I gone to the poor standard internet cafés, this book would have not been created. I praised the internet café owner about his good service, and told him to stay that way. Personally, I found a huge difference in internet search results while browsing in high-speed internet cafés and that displayed in poor-standard Cafés. In good-quality internet parlors, the quality of search and the connections you get is awesome, but you will encounter frequent interruptions such as system rebooting, system hang up, etc. in low-standard cafés. From that day, I stopped going to sub-standard internet cafés. The point is you have to hook up with the right environment, right people, and right tools to get right results. So take time to find the right environment.

> You are the product of your environment. So choose the environment that will best develop you toward your objective . . .
>
> —Clement Stone

Find the environment where you thrive. We would probably never heard of Tiger Woods if there were no golf courses.

—Robert Kiyosaki

Sometimes, the fastest way to change and improve yourself is simply to change your environment.

—Robert Kiyosaki

METHODICAL BARRIERS

(ix) Reading

Previously, I mentioned "not having reading or listening habit" as a barrier. Now I'm saying "reading" itself as a barrier. Am I contradicting my statement? No. To develop reading habit is to help you pick up good writing styles in English, or to help you become aware of good English communication.

Here I'm talking about reading as the one "how to way" to learn. For example, you cannot ride a bicycle by reading a "how to ride a bicycle" book. You have to get a cycle, sit on top of it, and press the pedal to start riding. I'm not in any way undermining the habit of reading. All I'm saying is this: YOU NEED TO READ AND ACT, NOT JUST READ AND FORGET, which is normally the case in our academic exams.

... What I began by reading, I must finish by acting.

—Henry David Thoreau

Another problem with "reading" as a method of learning is that not everyone will learn using books. Each person has his own learning style. According to Howard Gardner, there are six different ways people will learn. Some learn by reading; some learn by doing; some do well with pictures; some learn well when concepts are backed by logic; some learn best when aided by music; some learn well in the company of others; some grasp well when learning is related to the natural things such as plants, animals, nature, etc. So if your natural style is learning by reading, don't forget to act. If your learning style is not towards books, learn in a way that suits your style.

(x) Listening to Lectures

Listening to lectures is an old way of learning, which makes learning dull. This is also a significant barrier because your speed of learning is greatly hampered. Listening to lectures is a passive process; unless combined with action-oriented tasks, you would only have some information in your head. How do you learn anything? You learn anything by doing.

> We learn to speak by speaking; we learn to run by running; and we learn to love by loving; there is no other way.
>
> —St Francis de Sales

> Learning is an active process. We learn by doing.
>
> —Dale Carnegie

If lecturing is minimal and involves creating awareness and encouraging students to do a lot of practice, then learning will sprint. Even though there are different styles of learning,

learning by doing is the best way because it helps you remember all that you learnt (or at least "most" of what you learnt).

> Tell me, and I will forget. Show me, and I may remember.
> INVOLVE me, and I will understand.
> —Confucius, 450 BC [*Emphasis added*]

Note the key word "involve" in this saying. The concept of "involvement" can best be appreciated if we take it in the light of the life of a Butterfly. We all know butterfly is beautiful, stylish and is available in many varieties and colors. When it starts its life it is a caterpillar, a worm-like ugly creature with lots of hairs around its body. Then it moves to another stage called Pupa, wherein the animal is not visible to anyone, as it is covered in a case called cocoon. One fine day, in a spurt of a movement it changes into a butterfly. In all this process, the caterpillar and the pupa never care about what others think of them, how ugly they appear to the world. They are busy EATING—they simply munch the good-quality leaves, and get the vital nutrients, which help their survival and their emergence as a new butterfly. Do they complain that they are ugly? Do they take criticism of the people around? NO. All they do is INVOLVING in doing what it takes to become a butterfly. They don't focus on the acne, the blisters, the boils, the pimples, the wrinkles, the spots, the fine lines, or the black circles. Their beauty secret is simple. They nourish themselves. My message in this point is: You got to INVOLVE before you can EVOLVE.

When I started learning Standard English, experts said, "It takes 7 years to become a good copyeditor". I get disturbed regarding this time frame of learning. But, as I was concentrating on learning, slowly this disturbing thought vanished. I was learning, learning, and learning, only to struggle and rise again. I had been referring to dictionaries, studying various manuals, getting hands-on experience in day-to-day jobs, and getting feedbacks from experts. One fine day, I was commissioned to edit some articles of a Major Reference Work. As I was working, suddenly my mind had all the connections; all the knowledge that had been gained suddenly worked together as a team. I could not believe my eyes that I was able to spot finer and finer errors in the writing, and my edits were going from good to better to best. When I checked back my time frame, it was exactly 7 years. I was in awe of myself. Wow! Finally, I evolved as a butterfly (actually, a good copyeditor). Without much difficulty, I was gliding from sentences to sentences, thrashing the barriers to clear expression.

The experts were right. It did take 7 years for me to become a good copyeditor. This time frame is generally the case for gaining expertise in any field. Had I get caught up with the time frame, I would not have learnt this far. Just like caterpillars, I was munching on some good stuffs (good books and manuals) that will greatly help me in becoming an expert copyeditor. So don't worry about how long it takes to learn English. Munch on your daily food. Eat the meat and greens. To evolve like Popeye the sailor, you have to involve yourself in eating the spinach. So INVOLVE, EVOLVE.

> Flow is about being completely INVOLVED in an activity for its own sake. The ego falls away. Time flies. Every action, movement, and thought follows inevitably from the previous one, like playing Jazz.

Your whole being is INVOLVED, and you're using your skills to the utmost.

—Mihaly Csikszentmihaly, *Flow*

Crossing your barriers

Obstacles are those frightful things you see when you take your eyes off your goals.

—Sydney Smith

Everything in life depends on your mind. Though we all live in an outer space, where we interact with a lot of other people on a day-to-day basis, much of what decides our life is what's going on the inside of our minds. Everything we see in the outer world can be taken away in a moment—your possessions, your friends and acquaintances, your status, etc. When you go through difficult times what sustains you mostly is what is on the inside of you—your belief, your convictions, your attitudes.

The most important conversations you hold in life are the ones you hold with yourself. Your inner dialogue is an important key to success.

—Unknown

If you have a strong mind, you can cure all your mental ill health—depression, worry, anxiety, negative attitude. All your negative emotions can be healed if you have positive mindset and I-can-rise-above-all-my-challenges attitude. If you are person of purpose, you can cross any hurdle that is standing between you and your goal.

> I only see the objective ... the obstacle must give way.
> —Napoleon Bonaparte

Money problems cannot be solved by money. You need a creative mind to solve your money problems because money is just an idea. People in the financial or business world know the common slogan that "it doesn't take money to make money". In this information age, many teenagers are proving that. Many are becoming technological wizards and in turn becoming millionaires. Now you have some of the world's best advice on mind, money, and people skills. You can heed to books written by experts and straighten your mind, change your poor money habits, and develop good people skills.

If your cultural or any other background is causing you problems in your English learning, you can find somebody of your background who had crossed those hurdles. Get to know them, and get help. If you don't have a good learning environment, find one—go to a library, a book store, a friend's house, or a good English-coaching institute.

> Whatever reason you had for not being somebody, there's somebody who had the same problem and overcame it.
> —Barbara Reynolds

> Do what you can, with what you have, where you are.
> —Theodore Roosevelt

Chapter 4

English Communication: Benefits or Job Prospects

If something is going to affect your life, it's best to know as much as you can about it.

—Donald Trump

Communication involves expression from a writer/speaker, and comprehension from the audience.

English communication has four modules: Listening, reading, writing, and speaking. Each of these modules can be subdivided into General or Specific. The "general" category includes ordinary or general topics, but specific category involves communication with a unique purpose.

The specific use of English can fetch a job in Call Centers, in advertising agencies, in Medical Transcription companies, in publishing houses, or in the aviation sector. With specific English skills, you can study anything on your own, can patent an invention, can go for higher studies in Anglophone (English-speaking) countries, can become an established lawyer, can host a great TV show, can serve as a vocalist in Disney productions or in Discovery channel, can step into the glorious Hollywood, or can act in the world-famous Shakespeare drama company.

Now we discuss about each module and the benefits or job prospects it provides to the English users.

Listening

> Listening is hard work. Unlike hearing it requires total concentration. It is an active search for meaning, while hearing is passive.
>
> —Alfonso Bucero

Many may say, what's there to speak about listening? I'm not deaf. I have a good natural ear. So, listening is natural.

What's there to learn in Listening? If you are person with one such an attitude, you are bound for more surprises.

The importance of listening can be understood well in the light of students appearing for IELTS. The first thing all the students going for IELTS talk about is: "I heard that listening is very tough. I don't know how I am going to crack this exam". The exam may require listening to various accents— UK, US, Australian, Canadian, or European. The students don't dread writing or speaking. They are quite familiar with those skills in their academic years. They are not quite confident of their listening because listening skills are not taught in schools or colleges.

In normal conversations, you may act as if you are Listening. What if you act as if you are listening in an IELTS exam? Sure, you will fail in that exam. Listening to answer questions require a prepared mind and careful attention.

The following chart illustrates the benefits or job prospects in industries that requires listening comprehension in English.

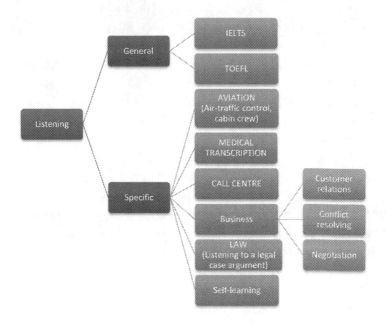

Reading

> The art of reading is the skill of catching every sort of communication as well as possible.
> —Mortimer Alder & Charles Van Doren

Students who are preparing for IELTS not only dread about listening, but equally dread about another aspect of communication—Reading.

Anyone who can recognize words can easily read newspapers or novels as a favorite pastime. This type of reading constitutes what is called "pleasure reading". But, most of us stumble in what is called "purpose reading" because it requires work, a lot of work. If you were given a task of writing assignments in your school or college, you need to read a lot. You cannot pleasure read any novel and write your assignment; you need to find resources relevant to your current topic, read them carefully, and need to take notes. How do you find out whether a person has good reading skills? Well, ask them about the summary of what they read. Good reading (Reading is actually listening with your eye) is evident by two things: picking up relevant information and retaining that information.

Imagine you wrote a small essay in your computer. What if your computer picks only one paragraph for processing and leaves the rest? What if your computer retains only a few sentences not the entire paragraphs? Well, you will say that the computer has some malfunction in information processing, and if you need to arrive at a decision using only those few pieces of information, the chances are more that your decision will be wrong. The beauty of computers is that they take in all that we put in, and give back (or show back) all that we put in originally. They are better than humans in terms of taking in a whole load of information and retaining them in their memory. Don't mistake me. I'm not saying humans are inferior to computers. The mere fact that such an extraordinary machine can be invented by humans shows the supremacy of human beings over this machine. The computers are merely tools we use to make our lives easier.

We may not be able to take in all that we listen or all that we read. (Sometimes this may be possible for people with extraordinary concentration power.) But we can keep sufficient pieces of information in our mind and retain the essence of everything we read. This is what good reading is all about.

If you ask somebody about a book they recently read, they say "yes I read it. It is a good book". If you ask the same person, what information from that book you retain? They will blink. If you ask children the same question, you will hear an amazing narration of stories after stories after stories. Young Children are like IBM mainframes: they handle information very well.

You cannot simply pump in more and more information into your computer beyond a certain point. Your computer, just like any other computer, cannot handle information beyond its memory capacity. Either you have to clear unwanted data or upgrade your computer memory to a greater capacity. The same goes well with our minds. This is the reason human beings differ in their earning power, status, social mobility, etc.—either they have to get rid of their junk or improve their capacity.

The following chart shows you the availability of jobs requiring English-reading skills.

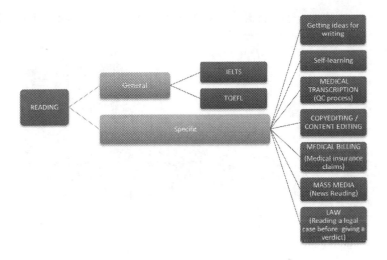

Writing

> Of all those arts in which the wise excel, Nature's chief
> masterpiece is writing well.
> —Duke of Buckingham Sheffield

Not all of us read books and not all of us listen carefully. But almost everyone writes. Right from our school, college, and until death, we all are expected to write in so many occasions. Leave letters, school and college assignments, Lab reports, report about a recent pleasure trip in outdoors, report about your recent visit to a local museum, letter to the bank manager for updating your address, letter to the airlines officer about your baggage loss in the airport, letter to the HR manager for reporting the loss of your ID card, letter to the editor of a local newspaper, condolences, applying for a job, writing invitations, writing "thank you" letters, or writing a will (estate planning) are some of the possible occasions where a person needs to write.

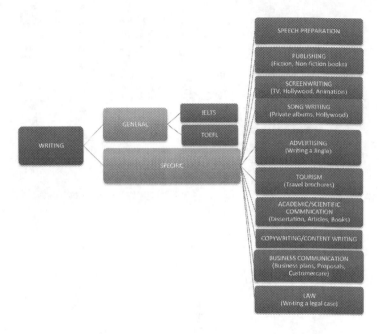

Because the writing needs are enormous, the job prospects of this module too are more when compared to jobs requiring reading or listening skills. The previous illustration shows the several career options involving writing.

Speaking

> Speak properly, and in as few words as you can, but always plainly; for the end of the speech is not ostentation, but to be understood.
>
> —William Penn

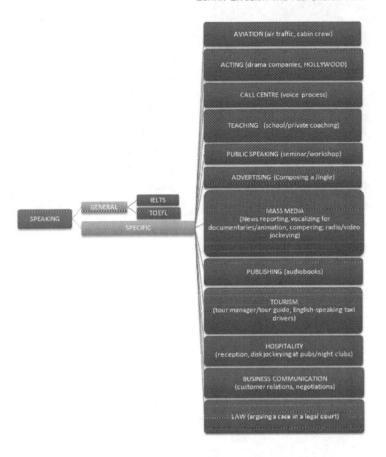

When compared to writing, Public speaking opportunities to a common man are little less. This may be because it is highly connected to leadership skills, and also because only a few would be chosen as leaders. Acting as the class representative or the class leader, lecturing a class, organizing a trip, addressing a crowd, acting as the student secretary of the school, giving an interview (if you are a celebrity), giving a business presentation, conducting a workshop, giving a demonstration in science exhibition are some of the occasions where people in leadership are supposed to speak.

However, there are occasions where almost anyone can speak. Speech competition at schools and colleges, Parents-teachers meeting, giving an academic seminar, participating in a debate, participating in a symposium, delivering a condolence speech, voicing your opinion through a TV news reporter, attending job interviews are a few circumstances that brings speaking opportunities to common people. The above illustration indicates a bouquet of careers wherein you can make your mark using your spoken skills.

PART II

METHODS

CHAPTER 5

What is the Best Way
to Learn English?

Learning is not attained by chance, it must be sought for with ardor and attended to with diligence.

—Abigail Adams

Learning is a habit

Learning a language is a HABIT. Just like other habits, learning involves REPETITION, that is, the practice of language on your part. Much more than the speed at which you are learning, it is the method of learning that is important. Understand the key concepts given in the book, and learn in a step-by-step manner and then expand your learning using any other source you may find. Another point I wish to suggest to all the aspiring English learners is this: achieve BALANCE. Learn English alongside your other roles in life—career, family, friends, your hobbies, your entertainment. Don't sacrifice any of these things and give too much emphasis on learning. Remember: *life is all about balance.*

Sounds form the basis of Listening comprehension and spoken language. Similarly, words are the rudiments of reading activity and written language. A person needs to listen a lot in order to master spoken language, and a lot of reading precedes skillful writing.

Children, via constant listening, learn a language without even knowing that there is GRAMMAR. Then they study alphabets and rhymes in the kindergarten, later on "words" and, further to this, grammar in schools and colleges. But the sad part is so many will run away the moment they hear the word GRAMMAR; so most of them swallow the ice cream instead of licking it one step at a time.

> One ought never to turn one's back on a threatened danger and try to run away from it. If you do that you will double the danger. But, if you meet it promptly and without flinching you reduce the danger by half. Never run away from anything!
>
> —Winston Churchill

By itself, grammar is not boring in any way, but the problem lies in how we are taught or how we learn it—are we going to SWALLOW AND SPIT? Or are we going to LICK IT AND ENJOY IT?

When a child sees the adult world, it constantly encounters sounds. It won't make any sense to the child initially, but after its brain cells begin to recognize the repeated sounds, it starts learning one word, two words, many words, much more words, hundreds of words, and thousands of words. If you are not a good listener (i.e. your listening comprehension is poor), and you try listening to Australian TV presenter, you would wonder what the hell is the person saying. (Initially, I found Australian accent a bit difficult to comprehend when compared to British or American way of pronunciation.) But if you persist in listening, your brain will recognize words that are repeated frequently, and slowly you can comprehend any accent—British, American, Australian or Canadian.

If you focus on listening for 20 to 30 minutes, and reading few pages every day, your speaking and writing will certainly improve. Even if you are not appearing for IELTS or TOEFL, practice all the four modules (reading, writing, listening and speaking), and you will become a good communicator.

> Resolve to edge in a little reading every day, if it is but a single sentence. If you gain 15 minutes a day, it will make itself felt at the end of the year.
>
> —Horace Mann

Cone of learning

Coming to the point of "What is the best way to learn?", now I would like to turn your attention to the following illustration called "Cone of Learning" put forth by Dale in 1969. This cone is the result of his study on the effectiveness of different types of learning in the education system. Since we are talking about the ice cream way to learn English, let us turn once again to the ice cream analogy.

Ice creams are traditionally served in cones. We have already talked about the ice cream (*9426GM* + *Grammar* + *Mix*), and now we talk about the cone (*the cone of learning*) that holds the ice cream. This cone, the cone of learning, was once an eye-opener for me, and I hope that it would be so for every learner. The cone of learning (for the cone of learning illustration, see www.millionaireacts.com/911/ways-of-learning-things.html) is summarized in the following list:

Active Involvement

1. Doing the real thing, simulating the real experience, doing a dramatic presentation constitutes the best way to learn a thing in an active way. These activities help a person to remember 90% of learning, after two weeks.

2. Giving a talk and participating in a discussion forms the second best way to learn a thing. Such activities help one to remember 70% of learning, after two weeks time.

Passive Involvement

1. Watching a demonstration, looking at an exhibit, watching a movie leads to the first best way to learn in a passive way. Such ways of learning help a person remember 50% of learning, after a period of two weeks.

2. The second best way in passive learning includes looking at pictures. This activity helps you to remember 30% of your learning, after a two-week period.

3. The third way in passive learning involves listening to somebody (e.g. lectures). You retain 20% of what you learn, after two weeks.

4. Reading comprises the final way in passive learning. After two weeks time, a person remembers only 10% of learning.

From the list, it is clear that the least effective way to learn is by reading and by listening to lectures—the two primary ways through which the education system teaches students.

On the contrary, the most effective way to learn anything is by actually doing the thing. The second best method to learn is simulating the real experience. Participating in a discussion or giving a talk forms the middle part of learning. These activities are far better learning methods than reading and listening to lectures. But, reading and listening to lectures is the only option available in most of our educational system; so, instead of trying to change the education system, learners can take time to do the actual thing—PRACTICING.

> Learning is an active process. We learn by doing.
> —Dale Carnegie

Remember to practice, in spite of how hard it appears or how many times you may mistakes. As Robert Schuller says, PRACTICE MAKES EVERYTHING POSSIBLE.

CHAPTER 6

Learn English the Ice Cream Way: Easy, Enjoyable, and Memorable

Life is like an ice-cream cone, you have to lick it ONE DAY AT A TIME.

—Charles Givens [*Emphasis added*]

The Ice cream way

Hardly, anyone would resist ice creams when offered. Almost everyone—young or old—likes eating ice creams. For some, eating mango flavor is a delight; Just the imagination of that whipped, bright yellow cream would stop their time. Others would prefer vanilla or butterscotch; still others treat themselves with black forest; a certain set would choose black currant or would indulge in combinations with cakes or aerated drinks; still few others experiment with a mix of flavors or would readily accept a single scoop of many different flavors just to relish their time.

Not only there are varieties of ice creams within a country, but there are ice creams unique to each country. Pistachio gelato is Italian in origin, Kulfi is an Indian ice cream, and Ais kacang is unique to Malaysia.

Just like these different flavors and different servings of ice creams, English too has many flavors or rather many colors. The scientific community would go for the flavor of

Standard English, the teachers would go for the academic flavor, advertisers would look for a creative flavor, lawyers go for the legal flavor, business persons like business flavor, and moviemakers want the screenplay flavor. It's the flavoring part that is different but the basic way to make ice creams is the same. If you took a good care of the basics of ice cream making, you can put any flavor or any combination of flavors to your heart's content. Whipping the ingredients well takes time—more time. But if you take things ONE STEP AT A TIME, the journey would be enjoyable, memorable.

English learning can be made interesting if we take it like eating ice creams. As I have already said, you can add any flavor you want but your base cream must be WHIPPED WELL, and the ingredients you add must be in a right proportion. That is, you may have a particular reason for studying English—you may want to become a writer, a lawyer, a copyeditor, a Call Centre executive, a TV presenter, or you may want to go to English-speaking countries for higher studies, or you may want to be involved in Disney productions or you may wish to write a fabulous screenplay script that will make a Box Office hit—but you need to keep your base laid well.

The various words, phrases and clauses, and grammar are the cream; the flavor to the cream depends on how you mix and use them. It is just MIX AND MATCH. Sentences are formed by mixing various words and by matching them to your imagination. But before mixing and matching, we need to know all about the cream.

Another principle in learning the ice cream way is to lick it ONE STEP AT A TIME—not rushing, not hurrying, not juggling, not gulping but relishing every lick.

> All things will be clear and distinct to the man who does not hurry. Haste is blind and improvident.
> —Titus Livius, Roman historian

All you have to do is learn a few things each day, concentrating on the one aspect at hand. Just like I evolved as a butterfly (actually a good editor), you will know one day that you have transformed from being a poor communicator to a master of words. Let us get started on how to take each step

> . . . Make a plan and chart the steps you must take to reach your goal. Take them ONE AT A TIME, and you will find that with each success the next step comes easier and easier . . .
> —Napoleon Hill [*emphasis added*]

As already mentioned, English language has two elements: *grammar* and *vocabulary*

It is mainly in vocabulary that the two major English variants exist: British and American English.

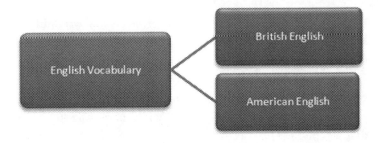

Now, remember my magical formula for learning English: **9426GM** (9 words, 4 phrases, 2 clauses, 6 sentence types) + **Grammar + mixing**

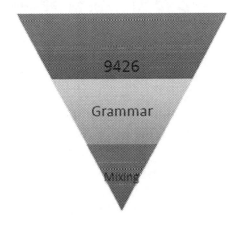

Let's see the 9426 first, then grammar and, later on, mixing.

Learning grammar vs. learning vocabulary

While learning English, many would be interested in learning vocabulary but not grammar. This again boils down to the "why"—the purpose of learning. I understand that this trend prevails because academic or civil service examinations in India put the candidates through tests on vocabulary skills and grammar. I guess that such exams may also exist in other countries (Anglophone or non-native English-speaking countries) because we are all under British rule, one way or the other. This trend seriously hampers English learning because most people study only vocabulary for the sake of cracking the exams but don't pay enough attention to grammar. In addition, learning vocabulary is comparatively easier than learning grammar. So it is natural that people prefer learning vocabulary rather than learning grammar.

The multiple choice format of these examinations makes the students (or job applicants) to have a "take it easy" attitude toward learning grammar. They feel that they can blindly tick an answer to grammar questions, and if luck works in their favor, they can crack the exam. If few people accidently and by luck cracked the exam, they will remain crippled in their communication for the rest of their lives, unless they learn grammar. Students please don't be angry with me for revealing your test-approaching secrets. My idea is that no one should remain crippled in English communication. You need to get the polio vaccination (the grammar) so that you can move, walk, dance, run, and sprint around your world.

Illustration of Poor English communication

Unless pressed by the need to crack those examinations, I would strongly recommend getting to know grammar first and then the vocabulary. I say "vocabulary" to mean learning more and more of interchangeable words or learning new, flamboyant words or bombastic terms. By learning vocabulary, many tend to think that "stomach" and "tummy" are interchangeable, but only a few people know that these words don't mean the same. Grammar is the foundation on which clear communication rests. Knowing only a few words but have adequate mastery in grammar will help a person communicate easily. Vocabulary can be learnt leisurely. If a person has poor grammar skills but have enough vocabulary in his mind can only make a mess of words, not conveying any meaning. This prevailing exam-cracking trend may be the reason that poor English communication abounds in many writings—in advertisements, in wedding cards, in academic writings, in college dissertations, and even in manuscripts submitted to the world-renowned Journals.

To amplify this thought, let me illustrate this with my experience of handling badly written, English texts: Please note that the names appearing in these examples are not real. The original names have been changed to hide the real identity.

Example 1. Office Circular:

<u>ORIGINAL VERSION</u>

BC/HR/CIR/14/2012
12th September 2012

Dear Staff,

Those who have referred candidates may submit applications for claiming referral bonus by 25th September 2012. The applications are to be submitted to Ms. Stephanie of HR department.

Regards

Chester Thompson
Senior Manager—HR & Administration

EDITED VERSION

> BC/HR/CIR/14/2012
> 12 September 2012
>
> Dear Staff,
>
> Please submit your application to Ms. Stephanie of HR department, by 25 September 2012 if you qualify for claiming the referral bonus.
>
> Regards
>
> Chester Thomson
> Senior Manager—HR & Administration

Though the original version of the letter is not wrong in grammar, it is a childish way of writing sentences. The two sentences in the original version appear very loose and the ideas are repeated unnecessarily. Maybe, the writer is a person who generally communicates in a "beat about the bush" way. See how concisely and clearly the edited version conveys the writer's message.

Example 2. Flyer (UK English: Handbill)

ORIGINAL VERSION

XYZ COMPUTERS
A Complete Computer Solution
Sale & Service
Contact: 8056128852

USED COMPUTER SALE

- INTEL Pentium IV Processor 2.4GHZ
- HP Invent Original Mother Board
- 512MB RAM
- 40 GB Hard disk
- CD Writer
- 17 inch LG CRT Monitor
- New Keyboard & Mouse

Just 6500—only

A to Z Software and Hardware services done by DOORSTEP at low cost,

All computer spare and accessories available.

Genuine is our professional name of service want to make your system Genuine call us.

<u>EDITED VERSION</u>

XYZ COMPUTERS
A complete hardware and software solutions company

Pre-Owned Computers for Sale
- 2.4 GHZ INTEL Pentium IV processor
- Original, HP Invent mother board
- 512 MB RAM
- 40 GB hard disk
- CD writer
- 17-inch, LG CRT Monitor
- Brand new keyboard & mouse

Rs. 6500/- only

Services offered at your DOORSTEP at attractive rates

All computer spares and accessories are available.

For genuine service, please call 8056128852.

The phrase "Complete Computer Solution" in the original version is wrong because the flyer is actually about a company (as stated in the edited version) and not about a solution. The word "sale & service" in the original version is unneeded and therefore it is deleted. "INTEL Pentium IV Processor 2.4 GHz" is an awkward phrase because the adjectives in this phrase are wrongly positioned. First of all, the computer is equipped with a processor—a fourth generation processor; an INTEL-manufactured, fourth generation processor with a 2.4 GHz capacity. So the correct phrase should be worded as "2.4 GHz INTEL Pentium IV processor" (for more information on the correct order of adjectives, see Ice cream 4, Lick 2).

Similarly, the phrase "HP Invent original mother board" has a wrong order of adjectives. The correct form should read as "original, HP Invent mother board". "Just" and "only" in the phrase "Just Rs. 6500/- only" mean the same. So "just" is deleted. In addition, there are other errors that the readers can easily spot by comparing the original and edited version.

Example 3. Wedding card

Original Version

You are invited

God decided our marriage in heaven and we would like to celebrate in earth with your pleasure company!!!

With weds of

Joy & Dreams

Me

K. Rohan

Weds

V. Sanjana

along with our parents invite you to share this day of happiness

Venue:
XYZ Community Hall, Chennai

Reception:
27 May 2012
Thursday, 6:00 pm

Muhurtham (Auspicious time):

25 May 2012, Friday, 6.00 am to 7.30 am

You are most invited
Make us Happy

Can you see the word "invite" is used three times in the original version? Moreover, few unnecessary words are used. Who is inviting is not at all mentioned in the original version. See the following edited version. Can you comprehend how clearly and concisely the edited version of the invitation carries the message? The original version seems ornate (with the word "You are invited" appearing in a special WordArt form), but has many errors; the edited version appears to lack ornamentation, but the message is clear and concise. Maybe, you can hire a good designer to put an effective design for this card. If you feel that the wording is bland, you may hire a good creative writer to provide an eloquent piece of writing.

Edited version

God decided our marriage in heaven and we would like to celebrate it with the pleasure of your company!!!

K. Rohan

Weds

V. Sanjana

We, along with our parents, invite you to share this day of happiness

Venue:
XYZ Community Hall, Chennai

Reception:
27 May 2012
Thursday, 6:00 pm

Muhurtham (Auspicious time):

25 May 2012, Friday, 6.00 am to 7.30 am

Example 4. Scientific edit

Original version:

Arhynchobdellid leeches **feed by either swallowing** their prey **whole** or creating a hemorrhage with their jaws and teeth**, and consuming** the pooled blood or **invertebrate body fluids**. Rhynchobdellid leeches feed by protruding their proboscis into host tissue, which is **aided** by **releasing** salivary proteolytic enzymes **at the tip**, and sucking fluid.

Edited version:

Arhynchobdellid leeches **either swallow** their prey or **create** a hemorrhage **in their host** with their jaws and teeth **to consume** the pooled blood or **the body fluids of invertebrates**. Rhynchobdellid leeches **protrude** their proboscis into host tissue (which is **followed** by **the release of** salivary proteolytic enzymes **at the tip of proboscis**) and **sucks the host's** fluid.

The clarity in the edited version is unparalleled when compared with the original version.

Learning vocabulary in an interesting way

Let's go back to our discussion on English vocabulary. According to Maxwell Nurnberg and Morris Rosenblum, the authors of the book *All about words: An adult approach to vocabulary building*, the problem with vocabulary building is not much about finding new words or finding their meanings, the problem is to remember them or how to fix them permanently in mind. One of the key concepts of this book is "memorable" (not "memorizing") way of learning. If you learn logically, learning will be interesting, i.e., learning will be enjoyable. If you enjoy something, they will be memorable (unforgettable)—they will automatically stay in your memory.

Even vocabulary can be learnt in an interesting way, not in a boring way.

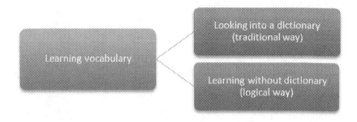

There are two ways you can learn a vocabulary: via dictionary or logical learning (using Etymology). The readers can consult books such as *Word power Made Easy* by Norman Lewis or *All About Words* by Maxwell Nurnberg and Morris Rosenblum. *If you know the root, you can easily find the shoot* is the approach used in the logical way of vocabulary learning. It involves knowing the root words of Greek, Latin, and French, and deriving the meaning of the word, without consulting a dictionary. Even though the logical way is the best way to permanently learn vocabulary, an intelligent approach would be to use both—maybe you can follow more and more the logical way and little less the dictionary way.

PART III

GRAMMAR

CHAPTER 7

What is Grammar? What it Does?

English grammar is so complex and confusing for the one very simple reason that its rules and terminology are based on Latin, a language with which it has precious little in common.

—Bill Bryson

The harmony between thought and reality is to be found in the grammar of the language . . . Uttering a word is like striking a note on the keyboard of the imagination.

—Ludwig Wittgenstein

Grammar: the cement that holds the words

As we have already seen, English has two elements: *vocabulary* and *grammar*. According to Oxford advanced learner's dictionary, grammar is defined as the rules in a language for changing the form of words and joining them into sentences. Grammar can help you arrange words but by itself cannot instruct you about how to write or talk well. A grammar can only teach you how to avoid mistakes and show you the right directions for practicing the language. Grammar is the cement of a language that holds the bricks of words in the correct order.

Vocabulary comprises all the words in a particular language. The words in a language are the result of the combinations of symbols, signs, or letters that have evolved to identify things and ideas. But words alone cannot make up a language. Imagine that you have all the words to express a message in three sentences, but have no method of putting them together, would it make sense? Of course not. Your attempt might look as shown below:

Business start up about what amount of capital will not take much capital not take little capital investment to know.

The process of conveying a message using words can be likened to building a solid wall using bricks. Bricks can be arranged on top of each other, but it cannot stay strong that way. Storms, heavy rain, or burglar attack can easily break down the bricks. So it is necessary to use a cement to hold the bricks together. The set of rules called grammar is the cement that holds the words together, and by using this you can create a sentence structure that can stand strong and convey a meaningful message.

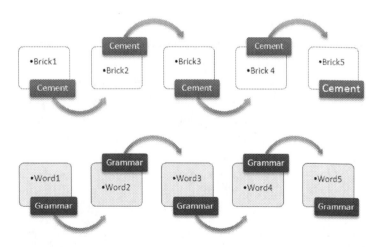

Illustration of the evolution of Grammar

Linguistics is shear servitude and drudgery until we have the joy of seeing order emerge from chaos.
—Robert Longacre

Dating back to the Greeks and Romans, English grammar consists of rules that helped the early users of this language to string their words together to create increasingly clearer and more complex messages. These rules enabled them to transform the messy, meaningless jumble of words into a meaningful sentence, as given in the following illustration:

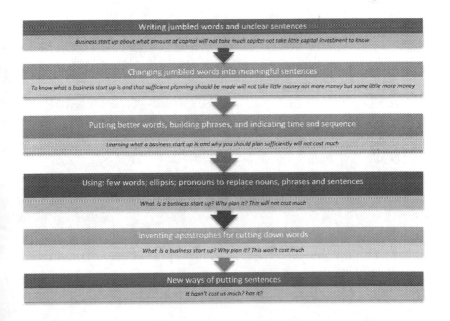

[Modified with Permission from Collins Good Writing Guide 2005, Hapercollins: Glasgow, UK]. Permission is pending.

To know what a business start up is and that sufficient planning should be made will not take little money not more money but some little more money.

Now the sentence is much improved when compared with the first example sentence, but it is still unclear. This calls for some more words and rules to make the message clear to the readers. The writer needs a better verb than *know*, such as *learn*. In addition, the writer needs to build phrases, and add inflections to basic words to indicate time and sequence: learn, learning, learnt. With these improvements the sentence becomes short and also expresses the writer's intention clearly:

Learning what a business start up is and why you should plan sufficiently will not cost much money.

Later on, the writer became smart by using few words to express the ideas instead of using more words, as in an earlier version. That writer also learned about ellipsis to avoid repetition of the same words, created pronouns to substitute nouns, phrases, and whole sentences. Now the sentence becomes two short questions:

What is a business start up? Why plan it? This will not cost much

And then, finally to make the message concise, the apostrophe was used, cutting out the need for one more word:

What is a business start up? Why plan it? This won't cost much.

Understanding the clarity of expression, we can bring out a trendiest sentence as follows:

"It hasn't cost us much, has it?"

This illustration may appear humorous to some of you or may be surprising to some others, but this is the way grammar might have evolved. This process of communication becoming better and better gives rise to an encouraging thought. It is not bad communication is our problem. But the problem lies in not refining our communication or rather not working out our communication. Just like there are several steps involved in the evolution of the most trendiest sentence we saw just now, our communication too can become better and better if we work at it. But some of us don't go beyond writing jumbled sentences. So those of you who are bogged down by poor communication, please don't stop there, but keep striving toward better ways of putting words together. Some day your messy sentences will become masterpieces.

Communication work for those who work at it.

—John Powell

CHAPTER 8

Words—The Parts of Speech

Words are, of course, the most powerful drug used by mankind.

—Rudyard Kipling

Words are the building blocks of communication, and English has 9 different words. All the English words can be grouped into 9 words—Nouns, pronouns, articles, verbs, adverbs, adjectives, prepositions, conjunctions, and interjections. They are called parts of speech. Remember: you need not have to memorize anything. Just be aware of the methods, concepts, and illustrations that are introduced. Refer them often, and they will stay in your memory.

Since we are talking of easy, enjoyable, and memorable way of learning, I would like to turn your attention to the following illustration (a poem) that explains the 9 parts of the speech in a clear way—the fun way. So don't see "parts of the speech" as old, dull grammar. Instead see them as a "poem". Don't memorize the 9 parts, but keep this poem in front of your study desk and refer it often, especially while writing.

Parts of Speech

Three little words you often see,
Are ARTICLES, *a, an*, and *the.*
A NOUN is the name of anything;
As *school* or *garden, hop* or *swing.*
ADJECTIVES tell the kind of noun;
As *great, small, pretty, white,* or *brown.*
Instead of the nouns the PRONOUNS stand
Her face, *his* face, *our* arms, *your* hand.
VERBS tell of something being done;
To *read, count, sing, laugh, jump,* or *run.*
How things are done the ADVERBS tell;
As *slowly, quickly, ill,* or *well.*
CONJUNCTIONS join the words together;
As men *and* Women, wind *or* weather;
The PREPOSITION stands before
A noun, as *in* or *through* a door.
The INTERJECTION shows surprise;
As *oh! how pretty! ah! how wise!*
The whole are called nine parts of speech,
Which reading, writing, speaking teach.

—Unknown

The idea behind classification is not just grouping but giving a name to each category. When God created so many creatures, Adam, the first man, gave each creature a name. When scientists conduct experiments, the first thing they do is to label or give names to the experimental groups. So whenever you encounter words, you should be able to identify what category a particular word belongs to—noun, pronoun, verb, adverb, adjective, preposition, conjunction, or interjection. Can you see that the 9 parts of speech are not gloomy grammar but a poem?

Let me share my story with the word "poem". As an Anglophile (English-loving person), I usually look to the advertisement hoardings while I travel within Chennai, the South Indian city where I live. One day, I came across a hoarding with a picture of a woman wearing an adorable sari (a long piece of clothing of Indian Women). The hoarding had the following words: IT'S NOT A SARI. IT'S A POEM ON YOU. For a lay person, a sari is just a woven piece of thread, but for a creative person, it is a poem about the women who wears it. See the power of creative writing! See the power of conciseness and clarity! It takes only two sentences to persuade the women to buy those Saris. Some of the World's most powerful messages are conveyed only in few words.

I saw the hoarding several years ago, but it still stays in my memory because it was interesting to me, and I was enjoying it. Do you get it? When you fall in love, it is easy to appreciate, and the things you appreciate will stay in your memory automatically. You need not have to memorize them. So if you start loving grammar, it will stay in your memory naturally, effortlessly. So this boils down to: how to turn the hatred towards grammar and make it appealing? Well, this is what the job of a teacher. This is what the book intends: how can grammar and other things be made appealing so that the people no longer hate grammar but embrace it, love it, and express it in words—beautiful words.

> Memorization is what we resort to when what we are
> learning makes no sense.
>
> —Unknown

Most of us are familiar about love stories or romantic movies. In those stories or movies, the guy (the hero) and the girl (the heroine) don't like each other at first because each does not notice anything appealing in them. But as days pass by, somehow, somewhere, someday one would notice something appealing about the other, and now the old hatred is changed to Love, and romance goes endlessly. So if you somehow, somewhere, someday find something appealing in grammar, you will start loving it and not hate it. And, you too can romance the language, and another sweep of Renaissance may take over. Like the person who wrote the advertisement words for the saris, you too will give out some of the finest pieces of writing or some soul-stirring speech that your audience will go gaga about it.

Coming back to the main point, I will introduce to you further simplification. According to Robert Day, author of Scientific English, the 9 parts of speech can be sub-classified into **name words, action words, descriptive words, and function words.** Remember: *the second magical formula is* **2133**. When you look at the total number of these sub-classified words, you can see that there are only 2 name words, 1 action word, 3 descriptive words, and 3 function words. So the 9 can be simplified to 2133.

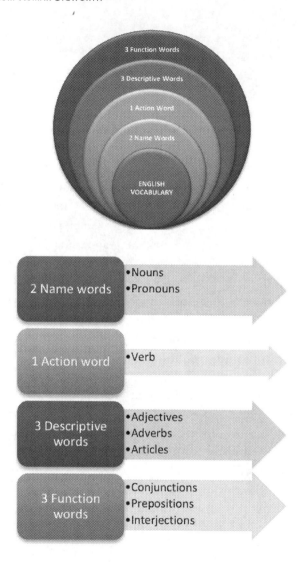

Now, we will see in detail all these sub-categorization of words.

NAME WORDS

There are two different name words: Nouns and pronouns. Nouns are the main players; pronouns are the substitutes of the main players. We see in detail about them as follows:

Ice Cream 1: Nouns

A noun is simply a word that describes a person, a place, a thing, or an idea. There are six types of nouns, but for simplification, we can classify them into three categories:

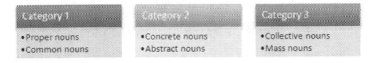

Generally, all English teachers would put common noun first and then the proper noun. But it is best to reverse the order. If you teach what a proper noun is, finding out common noun is easy—any noun that is not a proper noun is a common noun.

Lick 1: Proper and common nouns

A proper noun is a name word that indicates a specific person (Nelson Mandela), a specific place (Opera House), a particular thing (Maple syrup), or a particular idea (Globalization).

A common noun is any noun except a proper noun. If put simply, common nouns include a general type of person (student, musician), a general place (state, river), a general thing (book, building), or a general idea (fashion, humility).

Now you have two fundamental grammar rules. First, **proper nouns are always capitalized**, whereas common nouns are not. Second, proper nouns, because they are specific, are usually singular; **common nouns can be singular or plural**.

Lick 2: Concrete and Abstract nouns

Common nouns can be subdivided into two types: concrete and abstract nouns. Concrete nouns are those persons, places, or things that we can identify with our five senses (e.g. parrot, rain). Abstract nouns are ideas or qualities that cannot be directly perceived by our senses (e.g. freedom, kindness).

Lick 3: Collective and mass nouns

A collective noun, as the name implies, is a group or a collection of persons, places, things, or qualities (family, management, council, herd, committee, personnel). **The general rule is that such nouns are singular in form but plural in meaning**

> The country celebrates its independence this year.
> The family takes vacation this summer.

The first sentence can very well be rewritten as *The whole country celebrates its independence.* Here, the totality of a unit, irrespective of each member, is implied. Similarly, the second sentence can be written in an alternate form: The entire family (made of several people—the father, the mother, the first born, and siblings) takes vacation this year. So in both sentences, singular form of the verb is used.

But bear in mind that there are exceptions to this rule. **If the individuality of each member of a group is considered, plural form of the verb is used**.

> The country do not negotiate with terrorists.
> The family do not meet this year.

Here, the first sentence can very well be rewritten as We *Americans, as a country, do not negotiate with terrorists.* Similarly, the second sentence can be put in other forms:

> The members of the family do not meet this year.
> We, the family, don't meet this year, as we would normally do.

These two types of common nouns create a lot of trouble for English learners. The best way to deal with collective nouns is to decide whether the meaning is singular or plural. Let's go a little further with this concept. Consider the following examples:

A number of events were conducted.
The number of events conducted is 10.

In both the examples, the noun is "number", but the meaning is different—one is singular, and the other is plural in meaning. If I ask you, what were conducted? You would say "events were conducted". So the noun in the first sentence is plural in meaning. The meaning implied here is "several events were conducted".

Now, let's take the second example. If I ask you, what is 10? You would say, "it is the total number of events". So the second sentence can be rewritten as follows:

10 is the total number of events conducted.

To simplify further, the sentence can be put as "several events were conducted, and the total number of events is 10". Can you see that when logic is applied, meaning is nailed?

Lick 4: Function of Nouns

(i) Nouns usually perform some action or some action is done to them.

If a noun performs some action, it is called the *subject* of a sentence. A noun is called the *object* of a verb or of the object of a preposition if something is done to them.

Let's see some examples.

> Carlos threw the stone.
> Carlos threw the stone at the window.

In the first sentence, *Carlos* is the subject, *threw* is the verb, and *stone* is the object of the verb. In the second sentence, *Carlos* (the first noun) is the subject, *threw* is the verb, and *window* (another noun) is the object of preposition *at*.

(ii) Sometimes, nouns are not related to any actions. Instead, they define or characterize these nouns. Generally, in such sentences, some form of the linking verb "to be" is used.

> Naomi Campbell is a supermodel.
> Careebians are great athletes.

Ice Cream 2: Pronouns

Pronouns are words used as substitutes for nouns. Nouns are called "antecedents" when they are replaced by pronouns. Pronouns are one of the tricky things in English grammar because they can easily confuse the English users, especially writers. **The basic grammar rule regarding Noun-pronoun relationship is: the antecedent (the noun) and its pronoun must agree in number**. That is, if the antecedent is singular, pronoun should also be singular; similarly, with plural antecedents, plural pronouns need to be used.

There are 6 types of pronouns: *Personal, demonstrative, relative, interrogative, Indefinite,* and *reflexive* pronouns. Please do not memorize them. It is such a pain to do that. Refer the following chart often. If you are able to identify all these words as "pronouns" is enough to make a good communication. You need not have to go for sub-classification. When you learn to drive a car, you will be given certain instructions. Initially, you look for where is the gas pedal (UK English: the accelerator), clutch, and gear. Once you become proficient, you won't think of these things, but you simply drive.

> Don't be intimidated. Grammar books aren't as forbidding and textbooky as they used to be, and not all of them bristle with technical terms. You don't need to know the heavy terminology anyway. You can be a good driver even if you can't name all the parts of a car.
> —Patricia O'Conner, *Words Fail Me*

Similarly, when you learn or use English, you need to know to what group or category a particular word belongs. Knowing this will help you focus on the specific problem and find right solutions. Otherwise, you would not be able to fix your errors. Memorizing is not only a waste of time, but insanity. You can be sane and be intelligent.

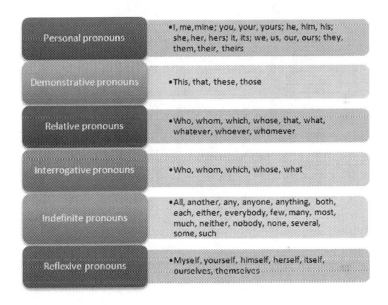

Personal pronouns	• I, me, mine; you, your, yours; he, him, his; she, her, hers; it, its; we, us, our, ours; they, them, their, theirs
Demonstrative pronouns	• This, that, these, those
Relative pronouns	• Who, whom, which, whose, that, what, whatever, whoever, whomever
Interrogative pronouns	• Who, whom, which, whose, what
Indefinite pronouns	• All, another, any, anyone, anything, both, each, either, everybody, few, many, most, much, neither, nobody, none, several, some, such
Reflexive pronouns	• Myself, yourself, himself, herself, itself, ourselves, themselves

Lick 1: Personal pronouns

A personal pronoun is used to substitute nouns referring to persons. What form of a personal pronoun is used in a particular sentence depends on how they are used in a sentence: as a subject, as an object, or as a possessive. There are 23 different personal pronouns:

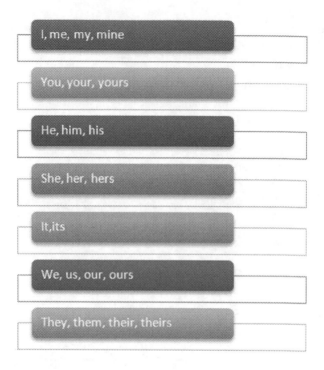

The common rule regarding, pronoun-antecedent is: **the pronoun must be close to the antecedent it substitutes**. Let's see few examples.

- ✓ Its skin is brown.
- ✗ It's skin is brown. [It is skin is brown.]
- ✗ Its not good grammar.
- ✓ It's not good grammar. [It is not good grammar.]

It is quite common that the possessive form of personal pronoun is mistaken. In addition, it gives an entirely wrong meaning, as shown in the following example:

✓ An eagle knows its prey. [The eagle finds its specific prey.]

✗ An eagle knows it's prey. [The eagle finds something as prey.]

Lick 2: Demonstrative Pronouns

These types of pronouns point out specific persons or things. There are only 4 demonstrative pronouns: this, *that, these, those*

Let's see some example sentences.

> This is my turn.
> That is a book.
> These will succeed.
> Those are sufficient.

Note: Demonstrative pronouns can also function as adjectives. As adjectives they are used before noun: that building, this car, these people, those seats.

Lick 3: Relative pronouns

This is a special category of pronouns because, in addition to replacing the nouns, they connect parts of the sentences. There are 9 common relative pronouns: Who, whom, which, whose, that, what, whatever, whoever, and whomever. They serve as subordinating conjunctions (see Ice Cream 7, Lick 2).

Winston Churchill, who served as the Prime minster of England during World War II, was truly a great orator.

Bear in mind that "that" can either be a demonstrative pronoun (see the relevant example under "demonstrative pronoun") or a relative pronoun. As a relative pronoun, *that* is frequently confused with *who*. *Who* should be used in place of people, and *that* is appropriate if used to replace animals or inanimate objects.

> The girl who came from Delhi did not perform well in the exam.
> I saw a church that was totally built of glass.
> Intuition is the amazing ability that helps us to make good decisions.

The word "that" can also serve as a conjunction, which leads to the never ending argument of *that vs. which* (see Chapter 10, Ice Cream 16).

Lick 4: Interrogative pronouns

Relative pronouns that help us ask questions are called interrogative pronouns. There are 4 common interrogative pronouns: who, whom, which, whose, and what. They are used to ask questions

> Who called me?
> What is this?

Lick 5: Indefinite pronouns

Pronouns that are used to replace nouns not referring to a specific person, specific place, or a specific thing are known as indefinite pronouns. They include:

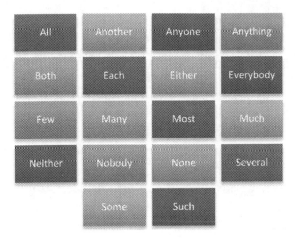

Now, we will see an example.

Anybody may go wrong, but we should not.

Lick 6: Reflexive pronouns

These are the least used type of pronouns, but they are often misused by English users. A reflexive pronoun reflects the action of a verb back on the subject.

She killed herself.

These pronouns should never be used either as a subject or as the object of preposition.

- ✗ Rubina and myself will go home. [Myself will go home.]
- ✓ Rubina and I will go home.
- ✗ He cheated Nazrul and myself. [He cheated myself.]
- ✓ He cheated Nazrul and me.

Consider the example sentences. Both sentences have two subjects. To make this concept easier, we will deliberately remove the first subject in each example. Now, the first sentence would read as "Myself will go home". No one on earth would write or speak this way. The correct form is "I will go home". If you want to use "myself" in the first sentence, you have to say: "I myself will go home". In this case, you convey others that you don't need anyone to go home. You can manage to go by yourself. Similarly, the second example would appear as "He cheated myself". You can say "He cheated himself" but you cannot say "He cheated myself". The correct form is "He cheated me".

Reflexive pronouns can also be used as "intensives". Such words are used to intensify the meaning or resolve.

> The minister himself visited the war-stricken people.
> We would rather do it ourselves.

ACTION WORDS

Next to nouns, most of the words in English are verbs.

Ice Cream 3: Verbs

Words that help us express a state of being or action are called verbs.

Lick 1: Function of verbs

It describes either the existence of a subject or an action done by the subject

Let's see some examples.

> Mozart is a great pianist.
> Temba reads books.
> The doctor examined the patient.

Lick 2: Types of verbs

All verbs can be divided into transitive or intransitive types. Transitive verbs transfer their action to an object (a noun occurring after a verb). Such transfer is needed for getting the complete meaning of a sentence. Intransitives do not transfer any action because there would be no object in the sentence, and the meaning would already be clear.

> Zohra offered me some soup.
> Lim died.
> They sat.

In the first example, the verb "offered" took an object (soup), and "me" is the indirect object in the sentence. If I ask the question Zohra offered what? The answer is soup or some soup. Without this object (the soup), the sentence would be meaningless. The second and third examples do not have any object; so they are intransitive.

Don't get confused now. Some verbs can be used transitively or intransitively.

> Sarath teaches French.
> Sarath teaches very well.

Now change the first sentence into a question: Sarath teaches what? Now change the second sentence into a question: Sarath teaches how? If the question requires a "what", you need an object. If the question requires a "how", you need an adverb. In the first example, *French* is actually the object of the verb *teaches*. So, the verb in the first sentence is transitive. In the second example, the verb *teaches* is followed by an adverb *well* and not by an object (noun). Therefore, the verb in the second sentence is intransitive.

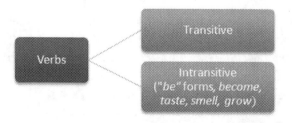

Linking verbs such as become, taste, smell and grow are frequently used intransitively.

> Medicine is a common term.
> She is bubbly.
> This smells good.

Lick 3: Variations of verbs

Verbs vary according to three things: *tense*, *voice*, and *mood*. Since we are talking about simplifying English learning, they are not discussed here. Instead, they are discussed separately in Chapter 13.

DESCRIPTIVE WORDS

Nouns or pronouns can be described or qualified by certain modifiers, and these modifiers are called *adjectives*. Similarly, verbs can also be modified. Such modifiers are called *adverbs*. Sometimes, modifiers can be modified; that is, *adverbs* and *adjectives* can also be modified by other adverbs.

Ice Cream 4: Adjectives

Adjectives describe a noun or pronoun.

Lick 1: Position of adjectives

Usually, adjectives come before the noun or pronoun (see the following example 1). Sometimes, they come after the noun and linking verb (see the following example 2)

> A Chinese man
> Mr. Cheung is a Chinese man.

Lick 2: Number of adjectives

Sometimes two or more adjectives qualify or modify a noun in a sentence

> A long brown jacket [two adjectives]
> A long brown soft jacket [three adjectives]

When there are more adjectives modifying a noun, it is better to check their order. Otherwise, the meaning will be unclear. See the following examples:

> ✗   Italian hot aromatic Pizza
> ✓   Hot aromatic Italian Pizza
> ✗   An investment private company
> ✓   A private investment company

Lick 3: Adjectival concept—Degrees of comparison

Adjectives can also be used with various degrees (positive, comparative, superlative) of intensity. Each adjective can be compared as in the following example:

Positive	Comparative	Superlative
•Hot	•Hotter	•Hottest
•Mild	•Milder	•Mildest

(ii) Not all adjectives follow the "er" or "est" endings occurring in comparative and superlative degrees. See the following illustration:

Positive	Comparative	Superlative
•Much	•More	•Most
•Bad	•Worse	•Worst

(iii) Sometimes regular adjectives can be modified without the "er" or "est" way, as shown in the following example:

Positive	Comparative	Superlative
•Cold	•More cold	•Most cold

Note: some English words cannot be compared; they are called "absolute" words. Examples include unique, perfect, exact, infinite. Certain things are either perfect or imperfect; they cannot be less perfect or more perfect.

Ice Cream 5: Adverbs

These are words used to describe verbs, adjectives, or other adverbs.

> She read hastily.
> PETRONAS tower is very tall.
> She walked very slowly.

In the first example, the adverb *hastily* describes or modifies the verb *read*. In the second example, the adverb *very* modifies the adjective *tall*. In the third, the adverb *very* modifies another adverb *slowly*.

All of us easily identify adverbs because of their "ly" endings. There are adverbs that don't end in "ly" (e.g. very) and cannot be easily identified (of course, you can use a dictionary to find out).

Lick 1: Confusion with adjectives

Sometimes English users easily confuse adverbs and their related adjectives. Take for example the adverb *really* and its related adjective *real*. It is a common error that people use *real* in the place of *really*, as shown below:

- ✓ Mary cooks really good.
- ✗ Mary cooks real good.

Similarly, see the following sentences:

- ✓ She works hard. [She is a hard worker.]
- ✗ She works hardly. [She generally does not work; she is more a fun-loving person.]

Lick 2: Adverbial concept—positioning of adverbs

The best way to deal with these descriptors or modifiers is to keep them as close to the thing they modify. It is similar to keeping the plate rack above the kitchen water tap. In doing so, the washing and keeping of the plates would be easy. Usually, there is no problem with the adjectives, but because adverbs can also modify adjectives, other adverbs or verbs, we need to be careful about where they are placed in a sentence. The most highly misused adverbs are *only*, *often*, and *never*. Writers who are not careful with these modifiers create confusion to the readers.

The placement being the main problem here, it leads to the need for the correct order of words to get the proper meaning of a sentence. This need leads to a new area of English grammar called Syntax ("syn" means together; "taxis" means arrangement). Remember: In every sentence, the subject (agent of action), the verb (action), and any modifier used to describe the subject or verb must be carefully positioned.

Imagine a public gathering. If you happen to see an important guest sitting in the middle row, what you will do? You, as the Party host, would gently persuade that person to sit in the front row. Important guests are to be seated in the front row. You need to do so with the adverbs or any other modifier. Keep them at their best place.

Positioning involves putting the right people in the right place at the right time.

—Unknown

Ice Cream 6: Articles

These are words that qualify nouns and pronouns. They are "a", "an", and "the". The "a" and "an" are called indefinite articles, and the "the" is defined as the definite article. "a" is used before words beginning with a consonant sound. The article "an" is used before words beginning with a vowel sound (a, e, i, o, u).

A place
A man
An apple
An Ostrich

Lick 1: Choosing the right article

The general rule in choosing between "a" and "an" is to go by the sound of a particular word not blindly by whether that word is a consonant or vowel. This rule goes well when placing an article before an abbreviation.

a Master of business administration degree
an MBA degree

Everyone would agree that the first sentence is correct. With the second sentence, we use "an" because we pronounce each letter not words. The letter "MBA" is pronounced "em-be-yeah", which initially gives a vowel sound.

Beyond logic, there seems to be some preferences in articles. The British tend to say *an* historian, but Americans prefer *a* historian.

Lick 2: Functions of articles

1. Articles serve an essential function in that it indicates whether a word is a noun or a verb. Because most of the words can function as both a noun and a verb. Let's see an example:

    Study progresses quickly.

Here the word "study" and "progresses" can be a noun or a verb. We all know "quickly" is an adverb. Without adding the article "the", the readers would wonder whether the study is progressing or the studies need to be quickly conducted to know the progresses.

    Study the progresses quickly.
    The study progresses quickly.

In the first sentence, "study" is the verb and "progresses" is the noun. In the second, "progresses" is the verb and "study" is the noun.

2. Remember that, in Chapter 8 (Ice cream 1, Lick 3), we saw that collective nouns take either singular or plural verb. This depends on which article is used.

    A number of scientists have arrived.
    The number of scientists who have arrived is 500.

Let's ask the question who have arrived? The answer would be "the scientists"; so a plural verb is needed. Similarly, what is this 500 stands for? The answer is the total number of scientists; so a singular verb is used.

It is said that articles appear easy, but mastering their correct use is difficult even for the native English speakers. When do you say "a mountain" or "the mountain"? There are no specific rules. You can have few guidelines, as in the following example. You say "a mountain" when you refer to any mountain; If you refer to a specific mountain (e.g. Mount Everest), you say "the mountain". You can't just say "mountain" without any article.

However, with plural nouns you cannot use the indefinite articles "a" or "an", but you can use the "the" to show that they are specific, but sometimes you can safely omit the definite article "the".

> The honey is sweet.
> Honey is sweet.

For a deeper level of understanding the articles, the readers are advised to refer to "article usage" by John Kohl and Susan Katz, which is available at www.rpi.edu/web/writingcentre.

FUNCTION WORDS

So far we have seen that English has *name words* (nouns, pronouns), *action words* (verbs), and *descriptive words*. These three are sufficient for writing a single sentence. A single, simple sentence is not enough for communication. We need to add complexities within a sentence so as to communicate complex messages. We need to have more name words or more action words or more descriptive words within a sentence, in order to make our communication beautiful. We have special agents for adding complexities in a sentence: *conjunctions* and *prepositions*. We are grouping here only conjunctions and prepositions as one category, but keeping interjections as a separate category because interjections won't help us in conveying complex messages but helps in conveying emotions.

Ice Cream 7: Conjunctions

These function words connect words or phrases (within a sentence) or clauses (between two or more sentences).

> Lisa and Audrey will be here. [Single sentence]
> He is neither in college nor in the park. [Single sentence]
> He failed, but she succeeded. [Two sentences joined by "but"]

Lick 1: Types of conjunctions

There are two types of conjunctions: coordinating conjunctions; subordinating conjunctions.

Coordinating conjunctions are used to show equal weights of the joined words, phrases, or clauses. There are 7 common coordinating conjunctions:

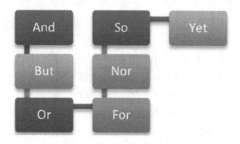

These common conjunctions play a major role in punctuation, which will be dealt with in Chapter 14.

Subordinating conjunctions connect unequal parts in a sentence. For example, they connect an independent clause with a dependent clause. Don't be afraid of these bombastic terms; you will learn their definitions and functions in Chapter 10.

Darlene watched a movie after she wiped the windows.

In this sentence, *after* is the subordinating conjunction connecting the unequal parts: a simple sentence (she watched a movie) with another unequal part (she wiped the windows). [Note: the clause following *after* is technically called subordinating (or dependent) clause]. This sentence is unequal in that "work" (wiping the window) is not equal to having "fun" (watching a movie). But consider the previous sentence "He failed, but she succeeded". Here, though there is contrast (one failed and one succeeded), there is an equality idea—both underwent an equal test.

Lick 2: Role of Subordinating conjunctions

Subordinating conjunctions often indicate time or a limiting factor. There common ones are as follows:

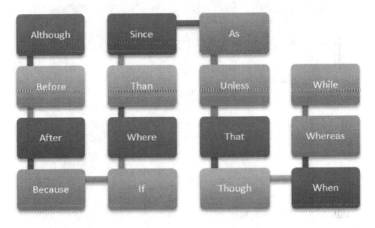

The following are few examples:

> Though he worked hard, he failed in the exam.
> Because we get stuck in traffic, we could not arrive in time.
> Unless we do something, the economic situation will
>   remain bad.

Lick 3: Coordinating conjunction vs. coordinating adverb

In addition to coordinating conjunction, there is another connector called coordinating adverb, which also connects independent clauses. Coordinating conjunctions are preceded by a comma, whereas coordinating adverbs are preceded by a semicolon and followed by a comma (see Chapter 13). They include:

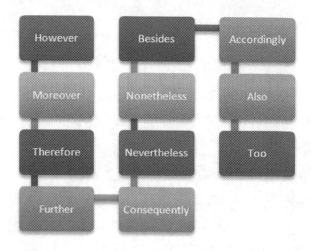

Let's see some examples:

He failed, but she succeeded. ["But" is the coordinating conjunction.]

We did not get the tickets; therefore, we couldn't see the play. ["Therefore" is a coordinating adverb.]

Ice Cream 8: Preposition

Prepositions are descriptive words used to join nouns or pronouns to form a phrase.

At the centre

Around the building

Toward the centre

The phrase formed using prepositions are called prepositional phrases (see Chapter 9, Ice cream 10).

Lick 1: Syntax problems with prepositional phrases

Writers usually have syntax problems while writing such phrases. Let us see an example:

- ✗ They offered an assortment of desserts for food connoisseurs with a background of music.
- ✓ For food connoisseurs, they offered an assortment of desserts, with a background of music.

Here the sentence gives a wrong meaning that the food connoisseurs (food experts) have an education in music. Actually, the meaning is the dessert is served in an ambience of music. See how a change in word order brings clarity.

Lick 2: Unnecessary Repetition of prepositions

Some writers repeat propositions, as in the following examples:

Inside of the house, there were many children.
This topic is outside of the scope of this work.

Inside, of, and outside, all are prepositions. The "of" is unnecessary repetition (this is quite common among American writing), and can be removed from the sentence.

Lick 3: Case of pronoun to be followed

The third concept relating to prepositions is the case of pronouns to be used when a pronoun follows the preposition. Prepositions are generally followed by objects. Thus they call for objective case of pronouns not the nominative type of pronouns.

- ✗ The fight was between She and I. [She and I are nominative case of pronoun.]
- ✓ The fight was between her and me. [Her and me are objective case of pronoun.]

Lick 4: Misuse of preposition to link an adjective

The function of preposition is to link a noun or pronoun, but some writers misuse prepositions to link an adjective to another part in a given sentence. See the following example:

- ✗ Californian red is too good of a wine to use.
- ✓ Californian red is too good a wine to use.
- ✓ Californian red is a too good wine to use.

The third sentence in the above example is written to help those who cannot comprehend the second sentence. Note that only the position of article "a" is changed in the third sentence. But, is there a difference in writing the sentence in the second way and third way? Certainly yes. They differ in the effect that is conveyed. The second sentence gives a heavy emphasis on the goodness of the wine (" . . . too good a wine . . ."), whereas the third sentence is just a bland statement (" . . . a too good wine . . ."). See how positioning is related to power!

It is generally said that in some tribal cultures, depending upon where you sit has some power. The same way with the words. A word sitting at a wrong place will only convey the idea in a bad way or will make the meaning of the sentence entirely wrong.

Lick 5: The famous rule—You shall not end a sentence with preposition

Most grammarians and many English teachers would shout at the top of their lungs when they see a sentence ending with a preposition. "You shall not end a sentence with a preposition" is a long-held rule. This rule is still used by many British people. But E.B. White says that ending a sentence with a preposition has its own effect, and you can easily judge by ear when to and when not to do it.

> There is nothing wrong, really with any word—all are good, but some are better than others. A matter of ear, a matter of reading books that sharpen the ear.
> —William Strunk & E.B. White, *Elements of Style*

Consider the following example.

Acceptable: It is the ice pick, not the knife, that he murder her with

Unacceptable: An ice pick, not a knife, was the weapon with which he murdered her

The first sentence, when read, gives a good sound to the ear. This is similar to a piece of music in which several instruments took part in their assigned role to make an eloquent musical flow that soothes the ear. A sentence sounding good to ear will also have a good flow. So a good-flowing and good-sounding sentence is what makes writing interesting. Grammar rules are guidelines to follow. Grammar is there to help us get the meaning of sentence clear. If following the rule does not help us grasp the meaning clear, why use it? So beyond using grammar, you need a good ear.

Ice Cream 9: Interjections

Interjection is a word, phrase, or sentence that conveys emotion

Alas!
How beautiful!
What a girl!

Chapter 9

Phrases

> Every single phrase is a string of perfect gems, of purest ray serene, strung together on a loose golden thread.
>
> —George du Maurier

Remember the 9 different words: nouns, pronouns, verbs, adjectives, adverbs, articles, prepositions, conjunctions, and interjections. Having seen all of those 9 words, let us move on to assembling them into phrases (Chapter 9) and clauses (Chapter 10). But, before doing that, let us see their definition.

<u>SIMPLE PHRASE</u>

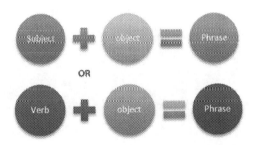

<u>COMPLEX PHRASE</u>

A phrase is a group of two or more GRAMMATICALLY-RELATED words that do not make a complete thought or meaning. In other words, a phrase is a group of words having either a subject or a verb but not both. Contrarily, a clause is a group of words containing both subject and verb, i.e., they make a complete thought or statement.

The key word in the definition of phrases or clauses is "grammatically related". If a phrase is related to a noun, it is called a noun phrase. Similarly, you can have verb phrase, adverbial phrase, etc. If we keep naming everything, the joy of learning and understanding will be greatly hampered. This is what happened with grammarians: they kept discovering names. Remember the whole point in writing this book is to simplify not to complicate. So if we take any phrase or phrases as just a group of words, it would be easy to use the language. So for easy learning, we see only 4 phrases: prepositional, infinitive, participial, and gerund phrases.

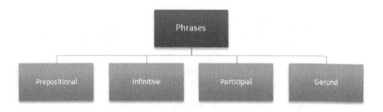

In framing these phrases into sentences, we need to focus on one thing: the order of each word in a sentence. This is what syntax is all about.

Ice Cream 10: Prepositional phrases

When a preposition, its object, and any words that modify the object are combined, the result would be a prepositional phrase.

For leisure, they went to the most famous and highly expensive resort in the country.

In this sentence, we have three prepositions (for, to, in), and therefore we have three prepositional phrases (for leisure, to the resort, in the country).

Lick 1: Punctuation in prepositional phrases

If a prepositional phrase occurs at the beginning of the sentence, you have to use a comma after the prepositional phrase.

Ice Cream 11: Infinitive phrases

An infinitive phrase is a combination of "to", a verb, and any objects or modifiers.

Lick 1: A Problem with Infinitive phrases—Split infinitives

> If you think a sentence will be more emphatic, clear or rhythmical, split your infinitive—there is no reason in logic or grammar for avoiding it. Some sentences seem better split than not.
>
> —Martin Cutts, *The Plain English Guide*

Similar to "you should not end a sentence with preposition" rule, most grammarians would say "you should not split an infinitive". But this once hard-and-fast rule can be broken now, if following the rule leads to clumsy sentences, as in the following examples:

- ✓ I fail to completely understand traffic rules. [The infinitive is split here.]
- ✗ I completely fail to understand completely traffic rules. [The meaning derived is: I totally failed not partially failed.]
- ✗ I fail completely to understand traffic rules. [The meaning conveyed here is: I totally failed not partially failed.]
- ✗ I fail to understand completely traffic rules. [The meaning of the sentence is: there are incomplete traffic rules.]

Ice Cream 12: Participial phrases

A participle phrase includes a participle (an "ing" verb used as an adjective), its object, and its modifiers.

Using the parts of speech, you can create infinitive varieties of sentences. Because a participial phrase functions as an adjective, it must do what an adjective does: modifying nouns or pronouns, and not other words. This also calls for the word order—or syntax.

Lick 1: Dangling modifier

If the participle in a sentence does not have any noun (subject) to modify, or when the noun is too far from the participle, the participle will dangle. This gives a new concept called "dangling modifiers", and you should avoid them in your writing. See the following example.

- ✗ Going to the beach, the Peggy's Cove was breathtaking.
- ✓ Going to the beach, I find Peggy's Cove breathtaking.
- ✗ Lying on the beach, my eyes got a glimpse of the rising sun.
- ✓ As I was lying on the beach, I got a glimpse of the rising sun.
- ✗ Flying over the Arctic, the harp seals are a breathtaking spectacle.
- ✓ Flying over the Arctic, you could get a breathtaking spectacle of harp seals.

The Peggy's cove (an iconic Canadian light house) is not going to the beach. It is there at the beach for people to come and visit. So the meaning is wrong in the first sentence of the first example. Similarly, in the successive two examples too, the meaning of the first sentence is wrong. "My eyes" are not lying on the beach. It is my body that is lying. Similarly, the harp seals cannot fly in an airplane; it is the humans who fly. With dangling modifiers, either we need to add the subject (noun), or we need to reword the sentence, as in the following examples.

- ✗ Going to the wilderness, my tire went flat.
- ✓ Going to the wilderness, I got a flat tire on my car. [The subject "I" is added in the second part of the sentence, leaving the first part unmodified]
- ✓ As I was going to the wilderness, my tire went flat.

Lick 2: Dangling participles with "it is" construction

Most participles dangle when the sentence following the participial phrase begins with "it is"

Going back, it is wise to take some rest.

Here the participle "going back" is modifying the "it", but "it" is not going home. The basic problem here is there is no subject in the sentence. This sentence should have been written as: *Going back, we must be wise enough to take rest.*

Lick 3: Present and Past Participles

Participles are parts of a verb. They are called that way because they participate in forming the verb. Such formation helps us to indicate time (tense) in a sentence. The participles with "ing" endings are called present participles; if the participles have "ed" ending, they are called past participles.

Considered as a great honor, military service should attract more and more youngsters.

Ice Cream 13: Gerund phrases

A gerund is an "ing" verb used as a noun. A gerund can be used alone, as in the following example.

Gardening is my favorite pastime.

A gerund becomes a gerund phrase when it is combined with an object. Gerund phrases are generally used as the subject of a sentence.

Writing a book is a time-consuming task.

Sometimes, gerund phrases can be used as objects

I enjoyed writing this book.

Because gerund phrases are naturally used in the correct place in a sentence, rarely they create confusion to the readers.

CHAPTER 10

Clauses

Sentences are like sharp nails which force truth upon our memory.

—Diderot

A clause is a group of words making a complete thought or statement. Unlike a phrase, it has both subject and verb. There are only two types of clauses: (i) Independent clauses; (ii) dependent clauses

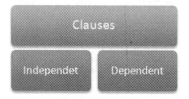

Ice Cream 14: Independent clause

An independent clause is a group of words that make a complete thought or statement, and they need to be connected to another clause. If it is not connected that way, it is called a sentence. Don't get confused. If an independent clause exists alone, it is called a sentence. If an independent clause exists in combination with another independent or dependent clause, it is called clause. I hope this concept is clear now.

Duncan is a hard-working student. [A complete sentence]

Duncan worked hard; he got an "A" grade in the exam. [Two independent clauses]

Duncan worked hard. He got an A grade in the exam. [Two complete sentences]

Having got good marks, Duncan got the scholarship for higher studies. [1 independent clause + 1 dependent clause]

Lick 1: Punctuating independent clauses

Independent clauses are usually separated from each other in three ways:

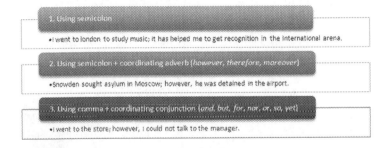

1. Using semicolon
   - I went to london to study music; it has helped me to get recognition in the international arena.

2. Using semicolon + coordinating adverb (however, therefore, moreover)
   - Snowden sought asylum in Moscow; however, he was detained in the airport.

3. Using comma + coordinating conjunction (and, but, for, nor, or, so, yet)
   - I went to the store; however, I could not talk to the manager.

Ice Cream 15: Dependent clauses

A dependent clause is as same as an independent clause in its structure (having both subject and verb) but it is introduced by a subordinating word. This subordination makes them dependent on another independent clause. So they are also called as subordinate clause. The subordinating words indicate either time (e.g. when, after, before) or doubt (e.g. if, whether)

If you exercise daily, you can live longer.

After you finish your home work, you can watch TV.

When daddy comes, he will give a handful of chocolates to you.

Whether the government is going to do something about the economic downturn or not, we can become creative entrepreneurs and change the economic situation.

In all these cases, the introductory subordinating words cannot stand by itself as a sentence. Take the first example. "If you exercise daily" is not a sentence, but whatever comes afterwards is a sentence. In order to distinguish the subordinating clause from the independent clause, a comma is needed. **So it is a rule that a subordinating clause should end with a comma**.

If you work hard, you will succeed; if you do a shoddy work, you will fail.

There are exceptions to this rule. If a subordinating clause becomes a subject of a sentence, it should not end with a comma.

That you are enjoying this dish is very likely.

Here if you remove the subordinating clause "that you are enjoying this dish", the sentence becomes meaningless. Here that rule cannot be applied, and therefore you should not put a comma.

This gives us a cardinal rule: You should never separate a subject from its verb with a comma.

In addition to serving as nouns, dependent clauses can function as adjectives, as in the following example:

We will all go as a team if we have to go.

In this example, the subordinate clause "if we have to go" finishes the sentence. If the same clause starts a sentence, a comma should follow as per the previous rule.

If we have to go, we will all go as a team.

There is an extension to this rule. **If a subordinate clause appears in the middle of a sentence, you have to use two commas to set it off from the main independent clause.** In this case, the subordinate clause becomes an interrupter to the flow of the sentence.

A busy person is a man or woman who, when living life, will not stop and smell the roses.

He, whom I have known from my childhood, came yesterday.

Note that, in the second sentence, the "whom" clause modifies the pronoun "he". This shows that the clause is adjectival, and the objective case of pronoun "whom" is correctly used. Nowadays, many English users prefer "who" here. They write: He, who I have known from my childhood, came yesterday. But, this is not correct.

See the first sentence. "Who" is part of the subject: a man or woman who… But you cannot use "who" here in the second sentence. The second sentence can also be written as: He came yesterday. I know him from my childhood. Here, you are using another objective case of pronoun "him". So the "who" is objective. You cannot say "I know he". So by writing "who" instead of "whom", you are making an object as a subject. Can you see that it is not just rules, it is pure logic that helps communicate clearly?

A common occurrence in this line of thought is that many authors would write a section called "who is this book for?" You cannot say: "This book is for they". You can only say: "This book is for those who . . ." or "the book is for them" (objective case of pronoun "they"). So the correct form is: "this book is for whom". This is the reason I have written the section title "For Whom this Book Is Written?" instead of the conventional "Who Is this Book For?" I believe this error should have crept into most casual conversations because it is easy to say "Who Is this Book For?" rather than "Whom Is this Book For?". Later on, this must have entered into the writings of many people and would have become so common that this error is unnoticed by many.

Please note that whenever a clause starting with "whom" occurs in the middle of a sentence, you have to use one comma before the clause and one comma after it.

Ice Cream 16: That vs. which problem

This concept revolves around a theme called restrictive and nonrestrictive clauses. If a clause in a given sentence is necessary to make a complete thought (otherwise, the sentence is meaningless), they are called restrictive clauses.

They are restrictive because they restrict the meaning of the sentence.

Banana is a fruit that is rich in phosphorous.

In this sentence, "Banana is a fruit" does not give much sense to adults (it makes sense to the pre-primary or primary kindergarten children). So the clause "that is rich in phosphorous" is essential to the meaning of the sentence. So this clause is restrictive.

Sometimes, clauses merely add a bit of extra information to a complete thought. In such cases, they don't restrict the meaning of the sentence. Therefore, they are set off with two commas.

Banana, which is rich in phosphorous, is truly one of the great tropical fruits.

Here, the "which" clause is not needed for the complete thought of the sentence? The sentence already is complete. The clause just adds more information to the already complete thought. So the "which" clause is nonrestrictive. Remember that this is not a strict rule. There can be exceptions.

For those of you who think why this "that vs. which" is that important, I would like to say that there is a world of difference in meaning between these two, and it is worth to make that distinction.

   ✗   Deoxygenated blood flows from the superior venacava that is located at the right side of the heart to other parts of the body.

   ✓   Blood flows from the superior venacava, which is located at the middle of the heart, to other parts of the body.

The first sentence with the use of "that" appears restrictive. But it gives the wrong meaning that there is another superior venacava located in the left side of heart. We all know that there is only one superior venacava, and it is located in the right side of the heart. So the second example with the nonrestrictive clause is correct.

> Green vegetables such as cabbage, raw banana and spinach are rich in flavanoids.
>
> Green vegetables, such as cabbage, raw banana and spinach, are rich in flavanoids.

Do all green vegetables have flavanoids? (as conveyed in second sentence) Or cabbage, raw banana, and spinach would only contain flavanoids (as said in the first sentence)? I don't know the answer. I leave it to the nutritionists. My point is that there is a vast difference in meaning. So writers do need to be careful when using them.

Chapter 11

Sentences

... A sentence should contain no unnecessary words, a paragraph no unnecessary sentences, for the same reason that a drawing should have no unnecessary lines and a machine no unnecessary parts . . .

—William Strunk, Jr.

So far we have seen all the 9 different words (parts of speech) that are necessary to communicate our thoughts. Now we have to do some "mix 'n' match" with these words to make a complete thought or a statement—the sentence.

Good communication rests on how clearly and logically you build sentences: words to phrases, to clauses, and to sentences. If you build sentences correctly, you can communicate clearly. If you make only a jumble of words, your words will have no meaning.

Anybody can mix the ingredients, but only the master chef can create signature dishes. Anybody can mix the milk, gelatin, cream, sugar, and other things, but only few can make ice creams as *Baskin Robbins* does. Similarly, anybody who studied using English-only curriculum (British equivalent: English-medium schools) can mix few words and write their thoughts, but only few can write as professional writers do. The difference is PRACTICE.

If you take any writing, you can find that there are only 6 types of sentences: questions, exclamations, and 4 other types of declarative sentences (simple, compound, complex, and compound–complex).

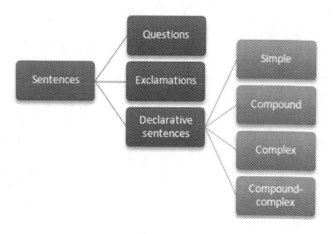

Let us see each of them in the following

Ice Cream 17: Questions

Any sentence that asks something is a question-type sentence. Such question-type sentences end with a question mark. But bear in mind that there can be exceptions.

> What do you know?
> What do you know is not the matter; it is who do you know.

The first sentence is a question, whereas in the second sentence, the question "what do you know" becomes the subject of the sentence. In such cases, you will not have a question mark.

Questions are generally asked to get a response. So question-type sentences are those that need a response.

How do you do that?

Sometimes, questions can be constructed to ask for a favor or to give a job instruction

Will you help me?
Would you get ready the report by tomorrow, please.

The first sentence is a question. The second is not. It is a declarative sentence.

Ice Cream 18: Exclamations

An exclamation is any sentence that shows negative or positive emotions. A question-type sentence will end with a question mark. Similarly, an exclamatory sentence will end with an exclamation mark. Exclamations can be words, phrases, clauses, or sentences, as in the following examples.

Beware!
At my count to 3!
Put it in the car!

DECLARATIVE SENTENCES

Ice Cream 19: Simple sentences

A simple sentence is composed of one independent clause—a subject, a verb, and sometimes an object.

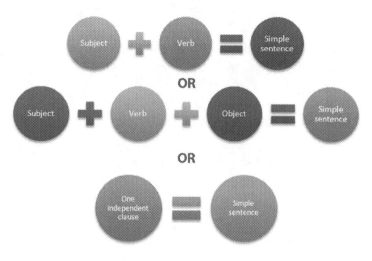

Let us see some examples.

> She gasped.
> He spoke the language.
> Nouns are name words.

Sometimes, a simple sentence may contain a predicate adjective along with subject and verb.

> She is beautiful.

Lick 1: Related concepts

A simple sentence need not always be short. Words, phrases, and clauses can be added to the subject, verb, or object in that sentence. Moreover, the subject, verb, or object in a simple sentence need not have to be single. There can be more subjects (a compound subject), more verbs (compound verbs), or more objects (compound objects) within a simple sentence. Let us see some examples.

> She ate. [One subject and one verb]
> He and she ate. [Two subjects and one verb]
> She ate and slept. [One subject and two verbs]
> He and she at and slept. [Two subjects and two verbs]
> She ate the chicken, the rice, and the dessert. [One subject, one verb, three objects]

Ice Cream 20: Compound sentences

A compound sentence is said to have two or more independent clauses.

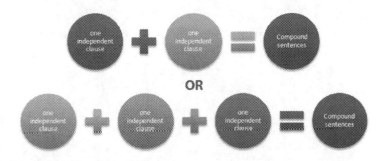

If two or more simple sentences have different thoughts, they need to be retained as separate sentences. However, if they are closely related, they need to be fused together—*Keep closely related sentences together*.

Lick 1: Punctuating Compound sentences

Two or more simple but related sentences can be combined in three ways:

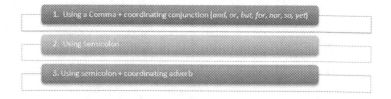

1. Using a Comma + coordinating conjunction (*and, or, but, for, nor, so, yet*)
2. Using Semicolon
3. Using semicolon + coordinating adverb

> The doctor diagnosed the problem, but could not cure the disease. [Case 1]
> The doctor diagnosed the problem; he could not cure the disease. [Case 2]
> The doctor diagnosed the problem; however, he could not cure the disease. [Case 3]

The first and the third show some connection by way of contrast. The second example is not showing a close connection (remember: a semicolon is a powerful separator but a less connector). In such cases, writers would use a dash or a colon.

> The servicemen found the problem—there is a breach below the engine.
> We cannot deny the fact: the evidence is strong against the suspect.

Lick 2: A common problem with punctuating compound sentences—the "comma splice"

You cannot join two independent clauses with a comma alone. Such a condition is technically called a comma splice.

- ✗ He sat, she ate.
- ✓ He sat; she ate. [No connection is implied.]
- ✓ He sat, but she ate. [Strong connection is implied.]
- ✓ He sat; however, she ate. [Strong connection is implied.]

Ice Cream 21: Complex sentences

A complex sentence consists of one independent clause and one or more dependent clauses.

Let's see some examples.

> When we are free from our debts, we will think our future again.
> When we are free from our debts, if we will ever are, we will think about our future again.
> Although she practiced well, she could not beat the defending champion.

Ice Cream 22: Compound-complex sentences

A compound-complex sentence is a combination of a compound sentence and a complex sentence. So it consists of two independent clauses and one or more dependent clauses.

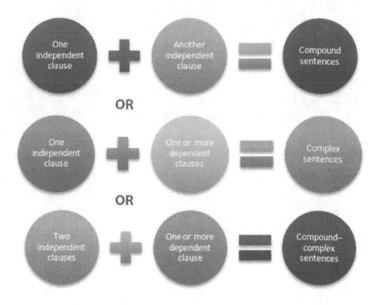

Moreover, all the rules that apply to compound and complex sentences also apply here. So it need not be difficult to understand, or to create, compound-complex sentences, regardless of how long the sentence may appear.

> Although she practiced hard, she could not win the match; in fact, she was defeated by the defending champion in two straight sets.

When I find time, I read good books; If I'm occupied with chores, I will listen to audio books.

Lick 1: Length of sentences

Generally, short sentences are preferred over long sentences. Being short alone may not make a sentence good, nor do long sentences are considered bad.

The new device can increase the longevity in aged population.

When the aged were experimented with the new device for 2 to 3 years, their normal functions were restored.

Long or short, if the words in the sentences are arranged in a correct order and they are punctuated correctly, sentences will be like solitaires set in a Jewel, reflecting the meaning with unmistakable sparkle.

. . . The setting of a word is just as restrictive as the setting of a jewel.

—William Strunk Jr. and E.B. White,
The Elements of Style

CHAPTER 12

Paragraphs

Paragraphs are not just chunks of text; at their best, they are logically constructed passages organized around a central idea often expressed in a topical sentence.
—Victoria E. McMillan

Paragraph is a composite unit of sentences revolving around a single theme. If closely related sentences are expressed and made into paragraphs, the reader would find no difficulty in following the writer's thoughts. With each new paragraph, the reader may get to know a completely new thought, or an expansion of an old thought, or a contrasting idea of a previous thought. So creating paragraphs is as important as making the correct word order in order to get the meaning right.

Ice Cream 23: Structure of a paragraph

Just like a speech having a beginning, middle, and end, written paragraphs should also have these three things.

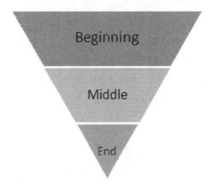

The beginning must clearly explain what the paragraph is all about. Then the sentences that follow should provide the additional supporting information regarding the subject of the paragraph. The end of a paragraph may provide a conclusion, a summary, or lead to a new thought (transition). Because the first sentence generally introduces the topic of the paragraph, it is called topical sentence. Similarly, the last sentence in the last paragraph ends with a conclusion. The problem is in the middle.

> The beginning of each paragraph is a signal that a new step in the development of the subject has been reached.
>
> —William Strunk Jr. & E.B. White,
> *The Elements of Style*

Sometimes paragraphs won't conclude something; they just give way to a new thought or thoughts, or to a transition of thoughts. When a transition occurs, the first sentence of the next paragraph should logically indicate to the reader that a transition will shortly be occurring. This can be likened to a signpost in a high way shouting, Hey! Look here. Hairpin bends are coming. Beware!

English has some words or phrases to aid us not to get loose track in reading. Let us see some examples. We have words and phrases indicating supportive information, contrasting information, and a conclusion, as given in the following illustration:

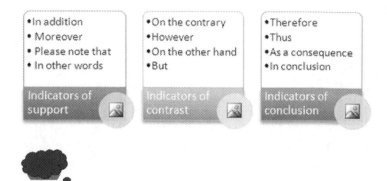

- In addition
- Moreover
- Please note that
- In other words

Indicators of support

- On the contrary
- However
- On the other hand
- But

Indicators of contrast

- Therefore
- Thus
- As a consequence
- In conclusion

Indicators of conclusion

Ice Cream 24: Length of a paragraph

Sometimes, we see paragraphs that are short; sometimes, we see paragraphs that are long. But, what is the rule to the length of a paragraph? The answer lies not in the length (of course, we should avoid having too long paragraphs) but in the previously stated logic: it should have the beginning, the middle, and the end. Put simply, each paragraph must convey a story—long or short but not too long.

You can tell a long story short, or you can tell a short story long, but the length is within the control of the writer.

Ice Cream 25: An example of a well-written paragraph

The following piece of text is taken from my article "why do we need teachers?" from my blog at http://mindtomanifest. blogspot.com.

Students are the assets of a nation. No nation can become strong if it doesn't have a well-groomed student population. If students are not molded, they become an eyesore for a nation. Every value, every good intent, and every goodwill starts at home; if not, they are groomed at school. No one can perfectly do that other than good teachers. This way good teachers are society changers and nation builders. Though the importance of teachers and teaching are portrayed by many, the following quotations embody them accurately:

A teacher affects eternity; he can never tell where his influence stops.

—Henry Adams

To me the sole hope of human salvation lies in teaching.

—George Bernard Shaw

The first sentence (the topical sentence) is about the "students" in general. The second and third sentences support the topical sentence. The fourth sentence transitions to value building at home. Followingly, the importance of teachers in shaping the students and their roles are emphasized. If the writer has new thoughts about teachers, a new paragraph may be started.

The first two sentences form the "beginning" of the paragraph. The third and fourth make up the "middle" of the paragraph. The last two sentences are the final thoughts or the "end" of the paragraph. Having all the three parts, the example text is truly a well-written paragraph.

CHAPTER 13

Tense, Voice, and Mood

Here's to the verb! It works harder than any other part of
the sentence. The verb is the word that gets things done.
Without a verb, there's nothing happening and you don't
really need a sentence at all.

—Patricia O'Conner, *Words Fail Me*

Verbs add drama to a random grouping of other words,
producing an event, a happening, an exciting moment.

—Constance Hale, *Sin and Syntax*

As already mentioned, Verbs vary according to three things:
tense, voice, and mood. But before going into those concepts,
we will see another basic way verbs differ. Depending on the
endings, verbs can be classified as regular or irregular. Regular
verbs have regular endings. For example, "watch" is a regular
verb with the past tense and past participle being "watched".
So verb forms whose past and past participles are indicated
by "ed" endings are called regular verbs. However, there is a
list of verbs which does not have the normal "ed" endings.
They are called irregular verbs.

Sometimes, the past and past participle of irregular verbs
may be the same, or they have entirely different endings. For
example, the past and past participle of the verb "bend" is
one and the same—"Bent". Contrarily, the verb "begin" has
the past form "began" and the past participle form "begun".
Sometimes, irregular verbs have the same forms to indicate

present, past, or past participle. For example, the verb "cut" is the same for present, past, and past participle. Now we will see tense, person, mood, and voice, each in detail.

Ice Cream 25: Tense

Verbs have different endings to indicate the time of action or the state of being. An action may happen, or a state of being may exist, in the present, past, or a future time. Basically, we have six different tenses, and we have the progressive form of those six different tenses. Collectively, they form 12 different tenses.

Lick 1: Present Tense

Verbs indicated in present tense express an action occurring at the present moment. In addition, they express an action that is said to be constant or generally true or said to occur regularly.

> The girl watches TV. [Present activity]
> I jog every day. [Regular activity]
> Sun rises in the east. [Constant activity]

Lick 2: Past Tense

When an action is began and ended in the past, that action is represented in past tense.

> The author finished writing his book.

Lick 3: Future Tense

Verbs in future tense indicate an action that will happen in the near or distant future.

We will attend the writers' conference.

Lick 4: Present Perfect Tense

Present perfect tense is used to express an action that was completed at an indefinite time in the past, or that began in past and continues into the present. You need to use "have/has + past participle" to indicate present perfect tense.

The desire for better life has kept the spirit of innovation throughout ages.

Lick 5: Past Perfect tense

Such tenses show an action in the past that occurred before another action in the past. You have to use "had ı past participle" to communicate your ideas in past perfect tense.

The rain had already spoiled the crops before they were harvested.

Lick 6: Future Perfect Tense

Future perfect tenses show an action in the future that will be completed before another action in the future. You need to use "shall have/will have + past participle" to write sentences in future perfect tense.

> The guests will have finished their dinner before coming back to the hotel.

Lick 7: Progressive Forms of Tenses (Continuous tenses)

All those six forms of tenses can have progressive forms. The progressive tenses show ongoing action in the present, past, or future. Be" form + present participle of the verb is used to form progressive tenses.

Present Progressive
They are practicing for their concert.

Past Progressive
They were practicing for their concert.

Future Progressive
They will be practicing for their concert.

Present Perfect Progressive
They have been practicing for their concert.

Past Perfect Progressive
They had been practicing for their concert.

Future Perfect Progressive
They shall have been practicing for their concert.

Lick 8: Shift in tenses

When you are writing about two different actions, avoid unnecessary shift in tense. In sentences with compound verbs, keep the tense the same.

- ✗ Each day the students meet at cafeteria and went to the library. [Unnecessary shift in tense]
- ✓ Each day the students meet at cafeteria and go to the library.

However, in sentences with two past actions occurring one before the other, you have to shift the tenses. If the first action is expressed in the past, use past perfect for the second action.

- ✗ They wished they finished quicker.
- ✓ They wished they had finished quicker. [necessary shift in tense]

Ice Cream 26: Voice

In addition to indicating tenses, verb inflections can also indicate a viewpoint of an action, known as the voice. If the subject does an action, the sentence is said to be in active voice. If the subject is acted upon, the sentence is said to be in passive voice.

Lick 1: Forming the passive voice

To form passive voice, You have to use a "be" form + past participle

Active: Christians proclaim a fast on Good Friday.
Passive: A fast was proclaimed by Christians, on Good Friday.

Lick 2: Improper and proper use of passive voice

In general, passive voice should be avoided because it makes the writing less forceful and less direct. Sometimes passive form makes the writing awkward, as in the following example.

- ✓ A believer believes God.
- ✗ God is believed by a believer. [The passive voice is awkward here.]

However, passive voice has its genuine use in sentences. When the writer wants to emphasize the action rather than the doer of the action, passive voice is the proper form to be used.

Passive: America was discovered by Columbus. [America is emphasized]

Active: Columbus discovered America. [Columbus is emphasized]

Although both the active and passive forms are correct in this example, it is the matter of emphasis that decides which form is appropriate. If the writer is very much concerned about America, passive voice is preferred. However, if the writer is interested about Columbus (the discoverer), active voice is the right choice.

Ice Cream 27: Mood

Verbs may also be used to indicate the writer's intention or a manner of expression in a sentence. Such intentions or manners form the mood of a sentence. Moods are of three types: indicative, imperative, and subjunctive

Lick 1: Indicative mood

The indicative mood expresses a fact or a question

> Another inflation is about to come.
> The upcoming government will not be able to solve the national debt.
> Will we ever be out of debt?

Lick 2: Imperative mood

The imperative mood is used to give a command or to make a request

> Be ready by 6 a.m. tomorrow.
> Meet me in the afternoon.

Lick 3: Subjunctive mood

The subjunctive mood is used to express a wish or a condition that is contrary to the fact

> If I were a minister, I would have taken actions for economic stability.
> If only I had born rich, I wouldn't be studying in a poor institution.

CHAPTER 14

Punctuation

> . . . Commas, colons, and semicolons can make our sentence not only clear but even a bit stylish . . .
>
> —Joseph M. Williams

Take a short text from any book. You deliberately remove every punctuation mark, including period. After doing this, try reading the text. You would realize how difficult it would be to read when there is no punctuation. So punctuation is a tool that helps us bring the right order of phrases, clauses, or sentences.

Punctuations are like signposts we see in the roads. Sometimes we encounter a school, a hospital, an intersection, or a dead end. According to each encounter, we have to take some actions. If a school approaches, we have to slow down; if a hospital is nearby, we should not use horns; if we encounter a 4-way road, we have to see both the sides before driving so as to prevent accidents; sometimes we have to stop altogether.

Similarly, a writer has to slow down the release of information; he or she has to keep the readers in suspense till the end, as in novels. Sometimes more phrases or clauses are embedded in a sentence, creating confusion. Sometimes the sentence has to end. Accordingly, the writer has to use an appropriate punctuation mark—a colon, comma, or a period.

There are 13 marks of punctuation in English: Periods, question marks, exclamatory marks, commas, semicolons, colons, dashes, quotation marks, apostrophes, parentheses, brackets, slashes, and hyphens.

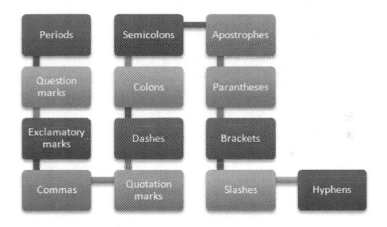

Punctuation marks can be grouped for simplifying English learning, as shown in the following illustration. This classification helps us to learn punctuation a little bit easier. Even though each punctuation mark is grouped under a specific category, some of them can fit into more than one group. That is, there can be exceptions. Forget about exceptions now. If basics are learnt well, exceptions can be easily understood. But learning exceptions may take time.

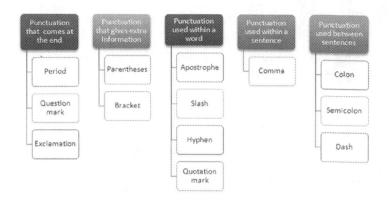

PUNCTUATION COMING AT THE END

Ice Cream 28: Periods

Periods (UK English: full stop or full points) are punctuation marks that help us to end a sentence. It is the strongest of all the punctuation marks because of its power to end a thought. It is similar to a big clashing sound in the drums that helps in ending a song. Periods have many functions. For simplification, we see only two functions.

Lick 1: Ending a sentence

When a sentence is a complete thought, a period is the appropriate punctuation mark to indicate its ending.

The statue of liberty is truly a masterpiece.

Lick 2: After name initials or after abbreviation

Periods can also be used to indicate a person's initials or abbreviations

> R.W. Emerson [Full name: Ralph Waldo Emerson]
> Sep.

Ice Cream 29: Question marks

When a sentence indicates a question, that sentence ends with a question mark. When a word or words in a sentence asks a question it is called a direct question. Such question sentences expect an answer.

> What is the best way to study English?

There are sentences that does not ask a question but indicate what question is asked. In such sentences, the question indicated is called an indirect question. So, a sentence with an indirect question does not end with a question mark, but with a period or full stop.

> Students asked me whether reading is the best way to
> study English.

A direct question sentence need not have to have more words. Even a single word can be a question sentence, as shown below:

> Who?   What?   Why?   When?

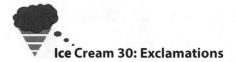

Ice Cream 30: Exclamations

Exclamation marks are used at the end of a word or a group of words to show some special meaning.

Lick 1: Indicating surprise, humor, or joy

Exclamatory marks can indicate surprise, humor, or joy.

> Surprise!
> Silly me!
> What a scene!

Lick 2: Indicating fear, anger, pain, or danger

Generally, fear, anger, pain, or danger can be expressed using exclamatory marks.

> Don't shoot!
> Damn it!
> Ouch!
> Help!

Lick 3: Giving orders

Sometimes, exclamatory marks are used to indicate making orders.

> Stand up!
> Stop!
> Call the police!

PUNCTUATION ENCLOSING EXTRA INFORMATION

Ice Cream 31: Parentheses (UK English: Brackets)

If you have a full sentence within parentheses, that sentence has to be treated like a normal sentence. That is, it should start with a capital letter and end in a period.

> This is where it ends. (It is here all started.)

If the information enclosed in parentheses is a fragment and not a sentence, then the enclosed information will be in lower case unless that information is a proper noun, and no period is needed.

> You need to know the ending (conclusion).

Ice Cream 32: Brackets (UK English: Square brackets)

Brackets or square brackets are the same as parentheses in giving additional information. Parentheses is used by the writer to give extra information about the writer's original thought, whereas brackets or square brackets are used to give additional information about someone else's original thoughts, and not of the writer's thoughts.

Lick 1: Indicating alteration or annotation to a quoted text

Brackets or square brackets are used to show any alteration or annotation to a quoted text

> The language [English] is perpetually in flux: it is a living stream, shifting, changing, receiving new strength from thousand tributaries, losing old forms in the backwaters of time.
> —William Strunk Jr. & E.B. White

Note the word "English" in square brackets, in this example. The writer has added this information to an already existing quoted text. If the writer did not add this information, the reader may not be able to understand what the word "language" stands for in this quote.

Lick 2: Giving additional information to another extra information

Sometimes, a writer may need to give additional thoughts to a piece of information already in parentheses.

(The cost was 6 ringgits [about 72 rupees].)

PUNCTUATION USED WITHIN A WORD

Ice Cream 33: Apostrophe

Apostrophes look like commas but are used in a superscript position. They are used to show possession.

Lick 1: Possession of singular nouns

Add an apostrophe and "s" to singular nouns to show possession

The book is called baby's cry.

Lick 2: Possession of plural nouns ending in "s"

Add just the apostrophe and not the "s" when you show possession of plural nouns ending in "s"

The doctors' strike came to an end.

Lick 3: Possession of plural nouns not ending in "s"

To show possession of plural nouns not ending in "s", use both the apostrophe and "s"

The Committee's approval.

Lick 4: Possession of persons whose names ending in "s"

When dealing with the names of persons ending in "s", add both the apostrophe and "s"

> Monica Seles's choice
> Dug Weiss's findings
> Douglas's shirt

Lick 5: Omitting letters (contractions)

While writing, apostrophes can be used to omit or leave out letters of certain words. This helps us to join words in a short form. Such words are called contractions. You can use contractions in informal writing (e.g. texting your message via SMS), but in formal writing they should be avoided.

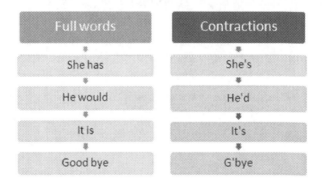

Full words	Contractions
She has	She's
He would	He'd
It is	It's
Good bye	G'bye

Lick 6: Omitting numbers

In addition to omitting letters, apostrophes can also be used to leave out numbers while writing. Such omissions of numbers are not allowed in formal writing.

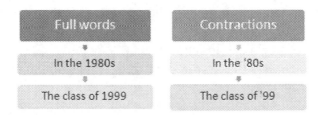

Ice Cream 34: Slash

Slashes are used to indicate "or" or "to". So it is better to avoid using this whenever possible, and tell exactly whether you mean "or" or "to". A/B means "A" or "B". Cost/benefit ratio means "cost to benefit ratio", which can be better written as "cost-to-benefit ratio".

In addition to these, there is a famous problem with Slash: "and/or" constructions in writing, which should be avoided. Most of the times, the "and/or" can be replaced with an "or"

  ✗   This helps me to meet and/or exceed customer needs.
  ✓   This helps me to meet or exceed customer needs.

Ice Cream 35: Hyphen

A hyphen is half the size of a dash, and is used to divide words at the end of a line in a printed material. In addition, it is also used to join words.

Lick 1: Forming compound nouns or compound adjectives

Hyphens are used to join two or more words to form compound words. Those words can be compound nouns or compound adjectives.

> Follow-up [Compound noun]
> Five-story building ["Five-story" is a compound adjective modifying the noun "building"]

Bear in mind that "Follow up" (without hyphen) is a verb, and "five stories" (without hyphen) is a noun, as in the following examples:

> You should follow up your customers via telephone or email.
> The building is five stories high.

Lick 2: Noun + participle or Adjective + participle

Hyphens may also be used to form Noun + participle or Adjective + participle compounds.

> Heart-felt thanks ["Heart" is the noun, and "felt" is the participle.]
> Blue-eyed boy ["Blue" is the adjective, and "eyed" is the participle.]

Lick 3: Forming group of words

Sometimes several words are linked together with hyphens to form a compound.

> State-of-the-art library
> Out-of-the-box thinking

Lick 4: Special compound words

Some special compound words are always hyphenated.

Father-in-law   Fathers-in-law
Sister-in-law   Sisters-in-law

Lick 5: Numbers and fractions

When fractions or two-worded numbers are used in writing, they should be joined by a hyphen.

One-third
Twenty-six

Lick 6: Avoiding confusion of compound words

When you leave some compound words without hyphenation, they cause confusion. In such cases, the readers have to figure out the meaning in some way. To avoid this, it is better to hyphenate the compound words.

An ant-eating animal is pictured in the book. [An "ant eater" is the subject here.]
An ant eating animal is pictured in the book. [An "ant" is the subject here, which is eating some animal.]

Now we will see another example.

✗   A bright red toy
✓   A bright, red toy [The toy is bright.]
✓   A bright-red toy [The red color is bright.]

The first sentence is confusing. While reading this sentence, the readers would wonder, what is bright? The toy or the color red? Aided by the right punctuation mark, the second and third sentences convey the meaning correctly.

Let us see a still more example.

- ✗ An old health professional
- ✓ An old-health professional [A doctor specializing in old people, called as geriatrician]
- ✓ An old health-professional [A general doctor who is of old age]

Lick 7: Normal word vs. prefix word

Sometimes a normal word and a prefix-containing word may have the same spelling but different meaning. To differentiate them, a hyphen is used.

Re-collect [collect again]	Recollect [remember]
Re-cover [cover again]	Recover [cured or withstood]
Re-sign [sign again]	Resign [give resignation]

Lick 8: Avoiding succession of same letters (especially vowels)

When a prefix ending and the following word has the same letter, a hyphen is generally used to avoid awkward sounding of a particular word

Re-echo [acceptable]   Reecho [awkward]

But there can be exceptions, as in the following:

Co-operation   Cooperation

Words such as "cooperation" were once a hyphenated word, but it is now accepted as one word. But still some people use "co-operation" as a hyphenated word. In general, it is better to refer to a dictionary before hyphenating a word.

Ice Cream 36: quotation marks

There are four main uses of a quotation mark: (i) to show the exact words of the speaker, (ii) to indicate a text borrowed from other sources, (iii) to set off the title of publications, and (iv) to give emphasis to a word or a group of words.

Previously, we saw that vocabulary differs between British and Americans. Quotation marks are a small area where Americans and British vary their use. In the Unites States, double quotation marks are used, and any quotation that comes within the main quotation is enclosed in single quotation marks. Contrarily, in the United Kingdom, single quotation marks are used, and any quotation that comes within the main quotation will be enclosed in double quotation marks.

Lick 1: Indicating direct quotations

Quotation marks are placed at the beginning and at the end of a direct quotation. Only the exact words quoted are enclosed within quotation marks.

> Sean Covey says, "The primary purpose of going to a college isn't to get a great job. The primary purpose of college is to build a strong mind."

You should never alter a quotation. If you are omitting a part of quotation, you can indicate that by using ellipsis. If you add any information to the quotation, that added material must be given within square brackets. Even a spelling mistake should not be corrected in a quotation. You can insert "[sic]" in a quotation to indicate that a wrong spelling appears in the original.

Lick 2: Quotation within a main quotation

To set off a quotation from the main quotation, single quotation marks are used.

"When Sean Covey said, 'The primary purpose of going to a college is to build a strong mind,' I was stunned," said the author.

Lick 3: Long quotations

When more than one paragraph is quoted, quotation marks are placed at the beginning of each new paragraph, and at the end of the last paragraph.

"_____
_____
_____.

_____
"_____
_____
_____
_____.

"_____

_____

_____

_____—."

Generally, in research papers or reports, quotations that occupy more than four lines on a page are usually set off from the main text by a 10-point indentation from the left side

[TEXT]

_____

_____.

[QUOTATION]

_____

_____

_____

_____.

[TEXT]

_____

_____.

Lick 4: Position of punctuation marks.

In addition to the quotation marks, British and American English differ in terms of placement of punctuation marks—whether inside or outside the quotation marks.

In the British system, if a punctuation mark is part of the original quotation, the mark goes inside the quotation; if a punctuation mark is not part of the original quotation, the mark goes outside the quotation. The following is the American system of punctuating the quotations.

I. Positioning periods and commas. Period or commas should be placed inside the closing quotation mark.

"What he is up to," he asked. She said, "He needs you."

II. Positioning semicolons and colons. Semicolons and colons are placed outside the closing quotation mark.

The boss said, "Get out"; so the workers went out in fury.
"Tring": the sign for the next patient to show up in the doctor's room.

III. Positioning question mark or exclamation mark. If the original narrator exclaims about or asks something, the exclamation mark goes inside the quotation mark.

He said, "where is the gun?"
She cried "Help!"

If the author or the writer exclaims about or asks something, the exclamation mark goes outside the quotation mark.

Did he ever say, "code red"?
I was excited when he said "I want 1000 computers"!

If both the original narrator and the author asks or exclaims, the question and exclamation marks go inside the quotation mark.

Did he ask, "where is the gun?"
In fear, I cried "Help!"

PUNCTUATION USED WITHIN A SENTENCE

Ice Cream 37: comma

Commas are used to indicate the readers to slow down, to pause, or to take a breath. It is the most highly used punctuation of all, and the most highly misused. Commas have such a large use that an entire book can be written about them. Since we are talking of simplifying English learning, we will see minimal uses of comma.

Lick 1: In a series (serial comma)

Use a comma after the "and" in a series of three or more items.

> You need pen, pencil, and paper.

In most British usage, a comma is not used before the "and" in a series of items. But, in most American usage, this series comma or serial comma is preferred. (I have used serial comma in this book.) However, in Britain, this comma is preferred in certain quarters, especially at the Oxford University Press. This is the reason this comma is also called as "Oxford comma".

Lick 2: Setting off interruptions

Use two commas to set off any interruptive words within a sentence.

> Harry Porter series, written by J.K. Rowling, is a best seller.

Lick 3: After introductory words

Use a comma after an introductory word, phrase, or clause.

> Unfortunately, he died in a car accident.
> Contrary to this, she recovered from the disease.
> If your work hard, you will succeed.

Lick 4: Between two unrelated sentences

Use a comma before the coordinating conjunction (and, or, but, for, nor, so, yet) that separates the two not very closely related sentences.

> This is the best plan and this is the most cost-effective
>   way to handle the problem. [closely related]
> This is the best plan, and you need to get the funding.
>   [not closely related]

Lick 5: After coordinating adverbs

Use a comma after coordinating adverbs (however, therefore, thus, moreover, or nevertheless) that join two independent clauses

> This is a best place to shop; however, the things are
>   expensive.

Lick 6: Single comma vs. double commas

You should never separate a subject and a verb, and a verb and an object, using a comma (If there are interrupters between them, they need to be set off using two commas not just with one comma.)

- ✗ I, myself will look into the matter. [Subject & verb is separated by a single comma]
- ✗ I myself, will look into the matter. [Subject & verb is separated by a single comma]
- ✓ I myself will look into the matter. [No interrupter occurs between the subject & verb]
- ✓ I myself, if needed, will look into the matter. [The interrupter between the subject & verb is set off using two commas]

PUNCTUATION USED BETWEEN SENTENCES

Ice Cream 38: colon

Colons are one of the punctuation marks used to tell the readers that "there is more to come after this". This means that whenever you see a colon, you need to look to whatever that follows—an explanation, an illustration, a list, or a summary.

Lick 1: Introducing a speech or a quotation

Colons help us to indicate a speech or a quotation in a piece of writing.

> She said: "It is raining".
> Remember the carpenter's rule: "Measure twice, cut once".

Lick 2: Introducing a list

Colons are used to introduce a list of things. The list can be part of the sentence (in-line list) or it can be displayed separately (display list).

Inline list

> We need to study four things so as to lead a successful life: mind, time, money, and people.

Display list

> We need to study four things so as to lead a successful life:
> 1. Mind
> 2. Time
> 3. Money
> 4. People

Lick 3: Introducing a summary

Colons can also be used for indicating a summary, a gist, or a brief of a piece of writing or a speech.

> The essence of his speech can be given in one word: Listen.
> He shouted: Help!

Lick 4: Introducing amplification or illustration

A colon is the tool we need to use to introduce an amplification or illustration of what has already been stated in the sentence.

The police finally solved the murder mystery: a mastermind killing people with an ice pick.

Lick 5: Colon vs. semicolon

Two sentences can be joined together using a colon or semicolon. However, the choice of colon or semicolon depends on whether the sentences are closely related or not. If two sentences are closely related, a colon is the correct mark of punctuation. If they are not related, a semicolon would be appropriate. Remember: colon is a connector, but semicolon is basically a separator.

- ✓ Hatred is like a slow poison: you don't see its effect soon but it is deadly. [Close relation is evident.]
- ✗ Hatred is like a slow poison; you don't see its effect soon, but it is deadly. [Close relation is lost.]

Ice Cream 39: Semicolon

Like commas and periods, semicolons are used to indicate a break or pause in writing. Semicolon is a punctuation mark stronger than a comma, but weaker than a colon. Sometimes, it can be used in the place of a period.

Lick 1: Between two independent clauses

A semicolon is used to separate two independent clauses.

I took her to the restaurant; we had candle light dinner.

Lick 2: Between an independent clause + a coordinating adverb and another independent clause

A semicolon is also used to join two independent clauses, along with a coordinating adverb.

> The economy is bad; however, the government can make reforms.

Lick 3: Breaking up of a list

A semicolon is called for when the sentence contains a list, and one or more item in that list in turn has a list.

> Sometimes we buy fruits; vegetables such as cucumber, cauliflower, and kidney beans; and mackerel, tuna, and chicken breasts.

Lick 4: Semicolon vs. period

A semicolon is equivalent to a period, but you cannot replace a semicolon with a period all the time. If the two independent clauses are related, semicolon is the right punctuation mark. Semicolon is a strong separator but a weak connector, whereas a period is the strongest separator of all.

- ✓ The movie starts with an umbrella; the heroine is introduced. [Close relation is implied.]
- ✓ The movie starts with an umbrella, and the heroine is introduced. [Close relation is implied.]
- ✗ The movie starts with an umbrella. The heroine is introduced. [Close relation is lost.]

Note: Even though the semicolon in the first sentences indicates a somewhat close relationship, it would be appropriate to use a colon to indicate a stronger relationship. Remember: *A colon is a strong connector than semicolon.*

Ice Cream 40: Dashes

Dashes are one of the punctuation marks overused by writers. Sometimes a pair of dashes can be replaced by a set of commas or parentheses. Brackets are the strongest dividers of words. They divide the extra information from the main sentence. Dashes are less strong than brackets, and commas are weaker than dashes. In general, if the word or words that you want to divide is closely related to the sentence, you have to use a pair of commas. If the word or words are not closely related, and the need for dashes cannot be justified, it would be safe to use parenthesis.

Lick 1: Announcing an appositive or a summary

A dash is uscd to indicate an appositive or a summary.

> You have to listen—really listen.
> Ice creams would make this meal complete—Black currant, Ferror Rocher, or Pistachio Gelato.

Lick 2: Indicating a contrast or surprise

A dash is used to indicate a contrast or surprise in sentences.

> The detectives pinpointed the murderer—the husband of the victim. [Single sentence]
> The thief snatched a gold chain from a women—the chain was found to be a counterfeit. [Two sentences]

Lick 3: Making an emphasis

A particular word in a sentence can be emphasized using a dash. In such cases, the word to be emphasized will be repeated.

> Our lives are full of mistakes—mistakes that could have been avoided if we would have listened to experts.

Lick 4: Setting off abrupt breaks in thought or interruptions in a sentence

Just like we may sometimes be interrupted in our speech, the writers may also get interrupted in their thought flow, and they deviate from the main thought. In such cases, dashes are used.

> When we are free from our debts—if we will ever are—we will think about our future again.

Lick 5: Avoid using more than a pair of dashes in a sentence

In general, avoid using more than a pair of dash in a sentence. Too many dashes will spoil the flow of the sentence and the easy grasp of the readers.

✗ Foul language—the kind you see on television—should be avoided—it pollutes the decorum of the school.

✓ Foul language—the kind you see on television—should be avoided. It pollutes the decorum of the school.

PART IV

ENGLISH COMMUNICATION

CHAPTER 15

English Communication: Listening, Reading, Writing, and Speaking

If I went back to college again, I'd concentrate on two areas: learning to write and to speak before an audience. Nothing in life is more important than the ability to communicate effectively.

—Gerald Ford

The number one criteria for advancement and promotion for professionals is an ability to communicate effectively.

—Ralph G. Nichols

The Power of Communication

Let us go back to the ancient civilizations. Imagine what could have happened if there is no communication? I believe *there would be no civilization without communication*. All that we are and all that we do is because we have been taught several things by several people. We learn a great deal of things because there is a medium of communication—the language.

What happens if there is a small group of people not capable of communicating anything between them? Slowly that tribe would degenerate and there would be no one left to represent that tribe. All the wisdom or any special knowledge gained by a particular person would have died when that person died. The lives of many ordinary people have gone from vapor to vapor. But few extraordinary lives goes from paper to paper (their writings are immortalized in print even though they too had to become mortals just like the ordinary people). History states that several languages have disappeared, and for some languages, there is no written form. It is no wonder that such people and their civilization diminished and finally disappeared from the planet earth.

Thank good heavens! Early men tried to communicate. They scribbled something in the caves, put some signs, learnt to use fire for cooking, and invented tools. So without language, the whole humanity would have disappeared from the face of the earth. We, human beings, all speak some languages; even animals speak their own languages. However, it is our ability to use written language distinguishes us from all other animals. It gave us the supremacy over all forms of life. Using language we could study and document vital information, share that information among us, and preserve it (in print or digital form) for future generations.

In war, the first thing an army does is to cut off supplies and communication lines of the enemies. See how vital communication is! The mere fact that I could write this book is the evidence that some time ago (two decades ago) I started learning to communicate in English and now having some mastery over it. What if I did not learn to communicate in English? I could manage to live a life, but all my potentials would have gone waste. This book would have not been published. To lose communication is to lose life—a rich life.

If you mention a name of a foreign country, the first thing comes to the mind is: What language they speak? Countries can be grouped according to what language they use. For example, all the French-speaking countries can be called as Francophone countries. Similarly, all English-speaking countries are grouped as Anglophone countries. Because England and France, the two great countries, ruled the whole word, their language still rules most of the affairs of the world. With English, not only certain countries are grouped, the whole world is grouped. (In studies of History, this grouping of a particular country or countries is called unification.) See the power of English!

As we all know, English language has four modules: Listening, reading, writing, and speaking. We have already seen the benefits and job prospects in each module of English language. In this chapter, we will discuss about what makes a good communication?—or more precisely what makes Good listening? What makes good Reading? What makes good writing? and what makes good speaking? I'm not going to write about what makes a poor communication or hurdles to good communication because if you focus on them, you will easily get bogged down by those barriers or hurdles. If I straightaway show you what makes a good communication in all those modules, you can easily focus on them and communicate well. OK, we will discuss each module one by one.

Listening

> Listening is hard work. Unlike hearing it requires total concentration. It is an active search for meaning, while hearing is passive.
>
> —Alfonso Bucero

> One of the best ways to persuade others is with your
> ears—by listening to them.
>
> —Dean Rusk

Listening is not the same as hearing. Don't be confused. Let me add more clarity to make you understand this concept. If you don't have any ear disorder or infirmity, you can easily hear. It does not require any action on your part. It is passive. It happens naturally. However, listening involves a tuned mind and a tuned ear. To put simply, you have to think and hear while listening, but you need to just hear while hearing. Listening is an active process because listening involves thinking, and thinking is an active process.

To understand listening better, I'll introduce a new illustration. Radio waves are transmitted all around us. But not all radio devices capture all information transmitted in the air at a given time. Because a particular piece of information is transmitted in a particular radio frequency, you need to tune your radio device toward that frequency. In other words, you need to readjust your device to match that frequency.

Poor weather, noisy surrounding, bad or faulty receiver all would muddle up the clarity of information reception. Sometimes, two or more radio frequencies that are close to each other would get mixed up, creating problems in reception. In such cases, tuning is not enough; you have to go for fine tuning. In general, the problems in communication may not lie in the speaker (the person who delivers the speech) or the transmitter (the device that enables mass transmission). It is quite common that the problems occur at the receiving end.

To improve communications, work not on the utterer,
but the recipient.

—Peter Drucker

Take for example the listening process at class room lectures
in a school or a college. The teacher or the tutor may be
enthusiastic, knowledgeable, and skilful in delivering the
message. But it is quite common that we could see students
suffer from poor reception of class room lectures. Such poor
reception may be due to a negative thought, a disturbing
personal circumstance, a recent unpleasant experience, a
personal struggle, a relationship problem, or a personal
financial turmoil. All these factors could easily muddle up
their receptivity of the message. The students may think
about these things and simultaneously listen to the lectures.
This condition is similar to too many messages getting
mixed up in too close frequencies, and the students would
pretend that they are listening but actually they may be day
dreaming.

9 out of 10 people daydream in meetings.

—Donald Wetmore

Good listening

To listen well is as powerful a means of communication
and influence as to talk well.

—John Marshall

Effective listening is engaged listening.

—Tom Peters

Well, let us go to the interesting point: What makes a good listening? Active listening involves arresting your unnecessary thoughts, turning away from all distractions, taking notes, gathering details from listening, paraphrasing your listening, and summarizing your listening. Finally, ask questions to reconfirm that you understood the correct meaning of the message—the meaning of the speaker not your own meaning.

Arresting unnecessary thoughts

> You cannot truly listen to someone and do anything else at the same time.
>
> —Scott Peck

You cannot be double-minded or several-minded while listening. If you think about several things while listening, nothing will get into your brain. If there is something bothering you, try to pin point what is the problem? If it needs your immediate attention, better attend to that problem rather than opting for listening. Alternatively, you can write about the problem: (i) What is the problem?, (i) How/when/where did it occur?, (iii) Who was involved? Having written your problem, now set your mind that you will attend to that problem a little later. Writing about your problem brings clarity to your mind, and you can easily arrive at a solution later. Be single-minded while listening; otherwise, you may lose vital information needed for your life.

> The mind will always be wandering. Just as when a chain is given to an elephant to hold in its trunk, it will go along grasping the chain and nothing else, so also when the mind is occupied with a name or form, it will grasp that alone. When the mind expands in the form of countless

thoughts, each thought becomes weak; but as thoughts get resolved, the mind becomes one-pointed and strong; for such a mind, self-inquiry will become easy.

—Sri Ramana Maharishi

Turning away from distractions

Factors such as uncomfortable clothing, lousy chairs, noise, heat, chillness, glaring lights, or other people's movement may distract you from listening. Deal with such factors intelligently.

Taking notes

This involves writing the speakers' ideas in your own words as you are listening. You may use shorthand, symbols, diagrams, grids, etc.

Gathering details

Unlike taking notes (wherein you will consider general information), gathering details involve capturing key ideas in some short form. If the speaker illustrates about a story, you can just capture that idea as a short title rather than writing about the entire story. The short title could be just "A and B" representing two key things or two key characters of a particular story: Alibaba & 40 thieves, or Economy & Entrepreneurship. So gathering details is about how intelligently and how quickly you capture the key ideas.

Paraphrasing

This involves writing the essence of what you listened in your own words, not copying word by word of what you listened.

Summarizing

See the whole picture of your notes, and then summarize the entire notes in few words. For example, this book has around 50,000 words. If somebody asks me to tell about the summary of this book, I would say as follows: Learn English like eating ice creams. If you rush eating ice creams you will have headache, but if you lick it one step at a time, you will enjoy it. Similarly, if you learn grammar one aspect at a time, you will enjoy learning English. The summary of this book is approximately 50 words. Those 50,000 words of the whole book can be condensed to 50 words.

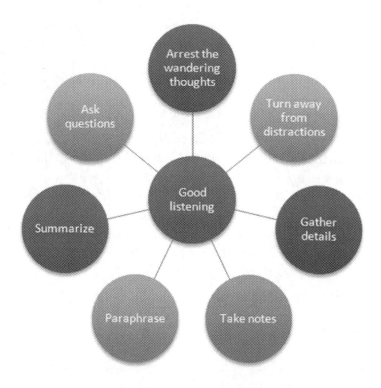

Questioning

Questioning is an excellent learning tool. Generally, communication ends with a question because either the questions or the answers to the questions determine whether the message has reached correctly. Whether it is a business conference or a class room teaching, asking questions is the normal way to close the communication. In IELTS exams, you are evaluated based on the answers you give to the questions once you finished listening, and not on your ear being checked by an ENT doctor and certified that you ear is defect-free. QUESTIONING AND ANSWERING ARE THE HALLMARKS OF COMMUNICATION.

> Who questions much, shall learn much, and retain much.
> —Francis Bacon

> A mark of having truly heard someone else is to respond appropriately...
> —Daniel Goleman

> There is no such thing as worthless conversation, provided you know what to listen for. And questions are the breath of life for a conversation.
> —James Nathan Miller

The reason we send acknowledgement emails is to indicate that we have received the message, and we got the correct meaning of the sender. Nodding your head, changing your gestures, and praising the speaker by clapping are acknowledgments confirming the reception of the speaker's meaning.

Generally, in any communication, the sender or the speaker sends one message, and the reader or the receiver confirms the sender's meaning of message. Sometimes, communication may not happen in a single time. When the original meaning of the sender or the speaker is not understood by the receiver or the listener, communication has to be repeated until the correct meaning is understood by the listener.

Americans: "Please, divert your course 15 degrees to the north to avoid a collision."

Canadians: "Recommend you divert your course 15 degrees to the south to avoid collision."

Americans: "This is the captain of a U.S. ship. I say again, divert YOUR course."

Canadians: "No, I say again, you divert YOUR course."

Americans: "This is the air craft carrier USS Abraham Lincoln, the second largest ship in the United States Atlantic fleet. We are accompanied by three destroyers, three cruisers, and numerous support vessels. I demand that you change your course 15 degrees north. That's one-five degrees north, or counter-measures will be taken to ensure the safety of this ship."

Canadians: "This is a light house. Your call."

Now, let's turn our attention to one more illustration before closing the "good listening" part. The above illustration is a transcript of radio conversation between a U.S. naval ship and Canadian authorities off the coast of Newfoundland. I could not find any other illustration that clearly emphasizes the importance of listening, real listening and not just talking.

Can you see the intense battle for the clarity in meaning?—the correct meaning, the meaning intended for the receiver. Can you see the Ego, the pride, the cockiness all muddling up the clarity in receiving the message? Had the people in the American ship remain proud and ignore the message or get a different meaning of the message, they would have destroyed their lives, and that beautiful well-built ship.

> It is impossible to speak in such a way that you cannot be misunderstood.
>
> —Karl Popper

> The biggest problem with communication is the illusion that it has been accomplished.
>
> —George Bernard Shaw

Poor listening or altogether the avoidance of listening costs a lot. Business problems, relationship problems, your schooling problems, or any other problem may be solved if at least one side of the party pays attention to listening. Sometimes people do listen well but they pretend because they do not want to face the truth, or don't want to face the consequences, or don't want to suffer some loss—loss of reputation, loss of money, etc. This is the reason "negotiation" is such a pain. You got to deal with idiots, some jerks, and some conmen.

Generally, youngsters won't listen to others. They feel that they are on top of the world (this feeling is good within some limits), and end up in problems. Parents, you can be patient with your teen children. Let them learn by doing— by committing mistakes. If they have to "touch the stove" to understand that it hurts, let them touch. Once they get their lesson, they won't touch it again.

Sometimes, parents don't listen to their children. It is a general truth that teens turning to substance abuse or to any other self-destructing habits generally stem from having parents not listening to them. Teens, if your parents don't listen to you, you need to be patient with them. You have to fight and get your message across until your meaning is clear to them.

> Few parents nowadays pay any regard to what their children say to them. The old-fashioned respect for the young is fast dying out.
>
> —Oscar Wilde

> If I were asked what single qualification was necessary for one who has the care of children, I should say patience. Patience with their tempers, with their understandings, with their progress. Patience to go over first principles again and again, steadily to add a little every day.
>
> —Fenelon

Managers don't listen to employees. They become prideful and haughty, and show off that they are superior to others. When their subordinates have a real problem, they turn deaf ears. The managers realize the problem only when employees give resignation. Sometimes, the subordinates won't listen. They become prideful because of their superior job skills and feel that they are irreplaceable. One fine day, after finding a suitable replacement, the management may tell them to leave their jobs.

How many neighbors have heartaches, pains, and hurts because one neighbor gives trouble to the other, and turn a deaf ear to genuine problems that need to be addressed.

When my financial life was in chaos, I listened to some Financial experts. I did not pretend that I don't have financial problems. I admitted my mistakes; I stopped my careless spending, and listened to them via my rigorous study on personal finance. I read the work of Robert Kiyosaki, Roger Hamilton, and many others. Slowly and steadily I could see my financial life on the right track.

Similarly, when I suffered from intense back pain, burnout, and stress, I listened to Joseph Bailey, who is an expert psychologist. He, along with Richard Carlson, wrote a beautiful book called *Slow down to the speed of life*. If not for the advice in that book, I would be continuing in my madness of overworking, and would put my life in misery. My well-being rested on LISTENING and so can be yours.

> There is guidance for each of us, and by lowly listening we shall hear the right words.
>
> —Ralph Waldo Emerson

Reading

> Reading, like no other medium, can transform your life in a flash, and you never know which book ... at which time in your life ... might be the one that rocks your world and inspires you to grow in ways you never thought possible.
>
> —Burke Hedges

Reading is not just viewing or browsing a text with your eyes. It is actually listening with your eyes. It involves scanning, comprehension, and reflection. Many of us go for pleasure reading: reading for enjoyment or entertainment. Reading comics, novels, or newspapers are some examples of reading as a favorite pastime. Some of us go for purpose reading: reading to find specific information. Reading for writing an assignment or for preparing a speech falls under purpose reading.

> If the first button of a man's coat is wrongly put, all the rest are bound to be crooked. Reading is the first button in the garment of education.
>
> —Giordano Bruno

Generally, all of us read more for pleasure than for a purpose. Since pleasure reading involves reading from beginning to end, even when we read for purpose, we try to do the same. There is nothing wrong in reading from beginning to end even for purpose reading. If you have the time, it is certainly good. But when you are pressed for time, it would be wise to do some intelligent way of reading: reading only necessary portions. If you are a writer, while reading for getting relevant information, you need to skip the bones and get to the meat so that your writing or speech will be loyal to your audience. If you are an author, Your ROYALTY from publishers depends on your LOYALTY to your audience.

To read effectively a large piece of information, you have to scan that information, pick up some details, spot the essential and nonessential parts, and read only relevant areas. Followingly, you need to take notes. If you read this way, you not only save time but would also read more and more information, which will help you finish your writing task quickly.

Good reading

> But if men are human because they can talk, they are
> civilized because they can read.
>
> —Dan Lacy

Good reading involves three things: (i) planning, (ii) reading, and (iii) taking notes.

Planning

Planning your reading is nothing but reading to get a general picture of a written text. If you are reading a short essay or a small article in a newspaper, you can go for catching some key words. If you don't find at least a few interesting things in a write up, that writing is not for you. You can quickly go to another source.

> A man's reading program should be as carefully
> planned as his daily diet, for that too is food, without
> which he cannot grow mentally.
>
> —Andrew Carnegie

Reading

If you are reading a book, take time to understand how it is organized (For example, this book is organized into four parts: background, grammar, methods, and conclusion), what is the central theme around which the book is written (For example, this book is centered on the "ice cream" theme), and what are the key topics addressed. You may also ask a few questions: Is the book user friendly? Does it have any thought-provoking quotations? Does it contain any pictures or illustrations? Does it have any interesting stories or examples? To put simply, planning your reading is nothing but KNOWING WHAT TO LOOK AND KNOWING WHAT TO OVERLOOK.

Reading involves catching the essence of the author's meaning. Read carefully and slowly, and reflect on your reading. As you read, your mind will make connections, and brings you thousands of thoughts. Carefully write all those thoughts because sometimes that idea may be lost forever. If you fail to write it, you may not have another chance to get it again. Personally, I missed a lot of my thoughts because I didn't pay enough attention to them. Nowadays when I get a thought, I will put that information in writing, irrespective of where I am and what I am doing. One time I got an amazing idea, but I don't have a paper or pen with me. At that time, I was walking in a suburb where facilities are limited and possibility of human contact is less. Suddenly, I picked up my phone and wrote the idea in it. One time, I wrote a piece of information at the back of a bus ticket. Nowadays I get a lot of ideas, but I'm wise enough not to let my ideas slip from me. I record them in some form.

> When out for a walk on your own, or when travelling, it is surprising what things can pop into the mind. Carry a note-book at all times and jot down straightaway what you remember or feel, because thoughts can slip out of the mind again as easily as they slip in.
>
> —Arda Lees

This book is originally an idea of likening English learning to Ice cream eating. When that idea flashed on my mind, I didn't write off this idea, but immediately captured the idea in my diary, and then started studying. The result is this book. How many good things have not come to fruition because we WRITE OFF our ideas rather than WRITE IN in a notebook?

> A new idea is delicate. It can be killed by a sneer or a yawn. It can be stabbed to death by a joke or worried to death by a frown on the wrong person's brow.
>
> —Charles Browder

Taking notes

Taking notes involve copying relevant information from a write up or writing the essence of information in your own words, which is called paraphrasing. There are several ways to take notes. You can use shorthand writing, a bubble diagram, or write a timeline notes (crystallizing your ideas in few words and arrange them chronologically). You can write a "cause and effect" note (organizing your entire ideas in the form of cause and effects: cause 1, effect 1; cause 2, effect 2, etc.), or go for a process list or a step-by-step note (writing your ideas in the form of either a computer programming or a biochemical cycle). Last but not the least, you can opt for a "KWL" strategy, as advised by Sebranek, Kemper, and Meyer in the book *Write Source 2000: A Guide to Writing, Thinking and Learning*. It involves arranging three quadrants or grids, and finding answers to the following questions: (i) What do I know? (ii) What do I want to know? (iii) What do I recently learnt or still want to know?

> One reads in order to ask questions.
>
> —Franka Kafza

Speaking

> A speech is poetry; cadence, rhythm, imagery, sweep! A speech reminds us that words, like children, have the power to make dance the dullest beanbag of a heart.
>
> —Peggy Noonan

Listening and reading are more to do with your comprehension skills, whereas speaking and writing deals more with your expression skills. In listening and reading, taking up information, understanding it correctly, and retaining it for future use are essential. However, in speaking and writing, delivering information, making it easy to understand, and making them retainable (memorable) for future use are essential. Listening and reading are required for a specific purpose: FINDING INFORMATION. However, speaking and writing are required for a completely different purpose: FINDING AUDIENCE. So, it is no wonder that we are instructed to ask the no. 1 question when planning a speech or any writing: Who is your target audience?

> Above all else, write for your intended reader; all that follows stems from this rapport.
>
> —Vincent Fulginiti

Good speaking

> The music that can deepest reach, and cure all ill is the cordial speech.
>
> —Ralph Waldo Emerson

There are four steps to good speaking: (i) planning, (ii) preparing, (iii) practicing, and (iv) delivering.

Planning

Planning involves finding the topic of the speech, the purpose of the speech, and the supporting details necessary to back up your point of view, your arguments, or to persuade your audience into some action. If you are clear about these areas and have sufficient and interesting information on these areas, you can be sure that half of your battle is won. Your purpose could be to provide a new information, an argument in favor of or against something, or a demonstration of either a "how to" thing or how something works. You, as a speaker, need to know the topic generically as well as specifically. For example, if your speech is about a certain specific method, you need to be aware of the other existing methods at least generally.

> Survey wide fields, but cultivate small ones.
>
> —An old saying

The supporting details that may be of interest to you and to your audience include: your personal experience, some facts, expert opinion, an excerpt from other resources, a picture, an illustration, a photograph, a chart, a pie diagram, a story, or a video.

Preparing

Preparing your speech involves writing a beginning, a good middle part, and an excellent ending. It is like song composing, wherein you have a prelude, an interlude, and an ending. You could start with a question, a fact, or a story. Or, you could guide the audience to imagine something (I have followed this technique in Chapter 1). You may also opt for reciting a famous quotation. Now I'll come to the middle part. You have to crystallize your ideas in a group of small cards and keep it for your reference. With these cards, you can easily narrate the middle part. Using an interesting fact/ story, providing a summary, sharing a final idea, explaining the importance of the topic are some of the ways to end your speech.

> Only the prepared speaker deserves to be confident.
> —Dale Carnegie

Practicing

Once you prepared a well-written speech, you need to visualize the actual scene of public speaking and start practicing. You could try talking alone in your personal room, you could talk in front of a mirror, you could talk using a microphone (and tape your speech, if needed) or take a video of your speech. Now the practice being finished, you can review your speech using the following questions:

- Did I speak at a right flow?
- Did I speak in a right tone?
- Did I speak naturally?
- Did I speak confidently?

Delivering

Having done this review, all you need to do is this: control your negative emotions (especially fear) and shoot toward the audience the arrows from your tongue, and don't stop until you hear a waving sound of applause.

> A flame should be lighted at the commencement and kept alive with unremitting splendor to the end.
> —Michael Faraday,
> in his advice to a lecturer.

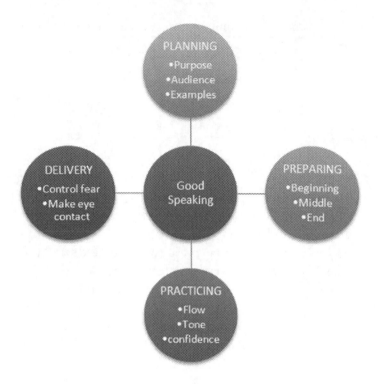

Writing

> Writing is an act of faith, not a trick of grammar.
> —William Strunk & E.B. White, *Elements of Style*

> Powerful writings are burned like a brand into the collective consciousness of a culture, even if very few people take the time to read those writings.
> —Burke Hedges

Writing is the supreme form of communication because it delineates us from other animals. I'm not in any way undermining the spoken language. Spoken language has its unique purpose, power, and charm. The power of writing can be likened to a ballistic missile; it can transcend continents or even time frame. For example, The Bible, writings of Greek philosophers, the Magna Carta (a legal document demanding rights to the citizens), Martin Luther's 95 theses, Shakespeare's plays and sonnets, the U.S. declaration of independence, the U.S. Constitution and the Bill of Rights, Communist manifesto (communist theories of Karl Marx), and Mein Kampf (philosophy of Adolf Hitler) all had a terrific impact on the whole world. (Note: Chennai residents can view the replica of Magna Carta in the Bronze Gallery of Government Museum, Egmore.) Except the last two, all made positive impacts. TV and satellite communication are recent technologies that could carry spoken word to greater geographical stretches, but written word is ancient and has its unique purpose, power, and charm.

> Spoken word leave impressions. Printed words leave tracks.
>
> —Napoleon Hill

Just like every big tree is once a tiny seed, every writing is once a tiny word, a tiny phrase, a tiny sentence, or only a tiny paragraph. In India, banyan trees are admired by many people. In the city of Chennai, a huge banyan tree was once considered as an iconic landmark of the area called Adyar. If you could see the seed of that tree (which is as tiny as an iota), you would be amazed at its full-grown status. The greatness and the vastness of its stretches are packed in an iota-sized seed. I believe the Americans admire a still greater and magnanimously huge tree native of California— The Giant Sequoia or Sierra redwood (*Sequoiadendron giganteum*). It is reported that one such a tree measured 243 feet tall and 60 feet wide, and it was nick named as "General Sherman". Readers of other countries can find their own native trees to make this concept more personal for them. If the seed is sown into the soil and watered well, the seed will give forth its shoots. If still a good care is provided, it will grow and become a gigantic structure, covering the skyline.

> Sometimes when I consider what tremendous consequences comes from little things . . . I am tempted to think there are no little things.
>
> —Bruce Barton

Similarly, if you take a good care of your idea and water it with your emotions and actions, soon your writing will give forth shoots. If you continue to take a better care of the rest of the writing process, your writing will grow hugely to be called as a book. Your shoots will become branches, buds, flowers, and ultimately fruits, which would be relished by your readers.

Good writing

> It is only when you open your vein and bleed on to the page a little that you establish contact with your readers.
>
> —Paul Gallico

> Writing isn't about making money or getting famous, getting dates, getting laid, or making friends. In the end, it is about enriching the lives of those who will read your book, and enriching your life as well.
>
> —Stephen King

In a nut shell, good writing involves six steps: (i) Framing a design, (ii) getting ideas, (iii) capturing your ideas, (iv) organizing your ideas, (v) writing, and (vi) revising.

The design

Beauty and functionality are the two sides of an innovation. There are countless inventions in the world that are proof for this statement. Many innovators have brought amazing solutions to problems via a clever design. We have fashion design, interior design, automobile design, architectural design, landscape design, etc. Apple iphone is an innovation by design and functionality. Vertical gardening is a breathtaking design brought out to meet the pressing need for greenery in what appears to be a dry, concrete land mass. It is no wonder that *need is the mother of all inventions.*

> Columbus didn't just sail, he sailed west, and the New World took shape from this simple and, now we think, sensible design.
>
> William Strunk & E.B. White,
> *The Elements of Style*

The metro subway system in Quebec City, Canada is another remarkable design. It is fashioned to provide a way to escape the harshness of winter. It is provided not just to commute but to live a life unaffected by the heavy snow. The Quebec metro subway has everything one could possibly want—boutiques, bookstores, and restaurants. The French Canadians or the Quebecois call the metro subway as "la Cité Souterrane" or "the subterranean city". Well, writing can be best aided by first having a design. If you cannot get a design at first, you can go for a free-flow mode and write anything and everything that comes to your mind. Writing in terms of cluster diagrams, having a mind map, or thinking in terms of a flow chart will aid you to arrive at a design.

Getting ideas

Reading is the gateway to get ideas, a lot of ideas. Read anything and everything you could come across in relation to the topic you have chosen to write.

> The greatest part of a writer's time is spent in reading, in order to write: a man will turn over half a library to make one book.
>
> —Samuel Johnson

> Read everything. Read! You'll absorb it. Then write.
>
> —William Faulkner

Think about your personal experience, get to know others experience, watch a movie, read articles, see a children's book, experience something in a new way. All these activities can reward you with rich ideas.

Capturing your ideas

Never forget to catch an idea. Writing an idea is a best way to capture it permanently. Remember the old saying: the palest ink is better than the sharpest memory. You may capture your ideas in a PC, a mobile phone, a tape recorder, or in a handy cam. It is not what medium you use that matters. It is how well you capture your idea that matters.

Never stop jotting things down that you see, hear, smell, etc. These things make great ideas or topics for freewriting and writing projects.

—Joe Strekall

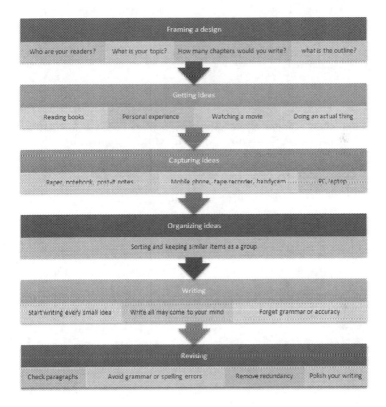

Organizing your ideas

Sort all your ideas into categories and organize them to sublevels would help you achieve clarity in your writing.

> Many people who have a gift of gab don't know how to wrap it up.
>
> —Lions Magazine

> It is important to be organized and to make things clear.
>
> —Kathryn Beasley

Start writing

Even if your thoughts are but a small trifle, start writing immediately. Don't stop the flow. Clear the surroundings of the trifle as best as you can, you could get gushing waters soon. Once you get a stream of ideas, start channelizing them. Don't stop until it is an overflow. Once you reach overflow, you may stop or continue to write as much as you want, and keep the excess for future use.

> I love first drafts. I just write and write. But I've learned that no matter how good I think my first draft is, it can always be better.
>
> —Emma Tobin.

> As you continue writing and rewriting, you begin to see possibilities you hadn't seen before.
>
> —Robert Hayden

Revising

Once the trifle become a mighty river, it is better to build a dam, and channelize the water for specific purposes. Sometimes the water needs to be contained. Sometimes it needs to be totally drained to avoid destruction to the dam. Sometimes only a few metric tons of water need to be released. Contain your ideas, drain them, or release only a small amount of them according to the need and place. Give importance to details. Check factual errors, poor grammar, poor sentence structure, bad flow, rhythm, etc. Polish your writing as much as you can until you are thoroughly satisfied with your writing.

> Revising is very important. It allows you to change things to make your piece of writing come to life.
>
> —Markelle Gray

> If all your sentences move at the same plodding gait, which even you recognize as deadly but don't know how to cure, read them aloud. You will begin to hear where the trouble lies. See if you can gain variety by reversing the order of a sentence, by substituting a word that has freshness or oddity, by altering the length of your sentences so they don't all sound as if they came out of the same computer.
>
> —William Zinsser

CHAPTER 16

Conclusion: A call for Action

The way to success is organized thinking followed by action! action! action!

—Napoleon Hill

Connectors [good communicators] inspire people to move from "know how" to "do now".

—John Maxwell,
Everyone Communicates but Few Connect

It is heartbreaking that millions of people don't know English, especially grammar. In many civil service examinations, either vocabulary or grammar or both are tested, which forms the basis of English language. The same is the criteria for selecting candidates for jobs in publishing houses, in Journalism, and in BPO organizations. We have come to the stage where the whole world is united by English. Now, English is the world language for commerce, science, teaching, computers, and air-traffic control. You cannot even think life today without knowing English. So it is necessary that we take English learning seriously.

Books on grammar are plenty in the book stores. Private English-coaching institutes are mushrooming around the world. But I could not come across any work simplifying English learning for the common man. I have searched in the major libraries in Chennai (the recently built, 27-crore rupees worth Anna Centenary Library; Connemara Library;

the British Council), in the top bookstores in Chennai (Landmark, Higginbothams, Starmark), and even on the internet. To the best of my knowledge, I could not find any solid blue print to simplify English learning in any of those resources. So I wrote this book.

I hope that this book will serve you as a guide to learn or to teach English in a simple way. You can add to this blue print any relevant things (especially grammar) from other sources and improve your learning. Even though this book gives you a glance in all modules of English communication, it is written especially for mastering written English.

Generally, the foundation of a building and even the big pillars of a building will stay strong in case of a storm or an earthquake, even though the structure of a building may be completely lost. If you lose the bricks but not the foundation and pillars, soon the building can easily be restored. Many "English-knowing" people also struggle in some minor or major part because the problem lies somewhere in their foundation. So getting your basics right is the need of the hour, whether you don't know English at all or you know some English.

Don't worry about the messes you may make. Every great sculpture is once a mess, a mess of meaningless clay. Do you remember the illustration of how grammar evolved? I'll once again present the illustration below for your easy reference and grasp.

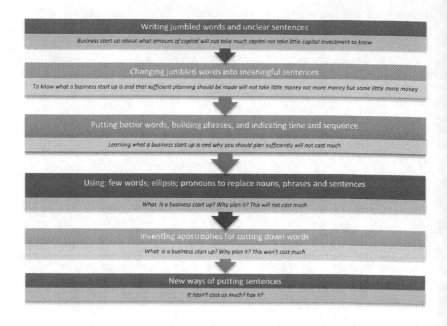

Initially, the words were in a mess, a mess of words not giving any meaning. As grammar is applied to them, slowly the most trendiest sentence evolved. So work on your messes. Who knows? Some masterpiece may evolve.

> Linguistics is shear servitude and drudgery until we have the joy of seeing order emerge from chaos.
> —Robert Longacre

Remember the sorting and keeping of words (9426), learn things one step at a time (have one ice cream a day and have one lick at a time), overcome your learning barriers, and learn the concepts and practice them. Above all, never, never, never give up! You are on your way to become a master of English language.

Well, eat a lot of ice creams! But one at a time. The following is a short poem I wrote to enthuse you to take action:

Take your PICK
And each time have a LICK
Know what makes you TICK
And make grammar STICK

Relish the ice creams, enjoy them, escape into them, go deep into them, and take time to live for yourself, for your loved ones, and for your community.

If you're a student, learn English this new way.
If you're a parent or a teacher, teach your children English this new way.
If you're a Government leader, especially the Minister of Education, interested in the welfare of your students and your nation, implement this new method of English learning in your school or college curriculum.

All the best! I'll finish the book with two thought-provoking quotes, which compels you to take action. Alright, take action.

My will shall shape my future.
Whether I fail or succeed shall be no man's doing but my own.
I am the force.
I can clear any obstacle before me or I can be lost in the maze.

My choice, my responsibility;
Win or lose, only I hold the key to my destiny.

—Elaine Maxwell

Whatever you can do, or dream you can, begin it. Boldness has genius, power, and magic in it. Begin it now.

—John Wolfgang von Goethe

APPENDIX I.
NOTES TO THE AUTHORITIES

Letter to the Honorable Ministers of Education worldwide

Dear Minister

Thank you for this opportunity to write to you on an issue that has far-reaching implications globally and locally—educating the children of your country in English communication. Whether you are a minister of a Native English-speaking country or of a country with English as an official or a second language, you cannot get away from framing policies on how English will be taught in the educational institutions of your country.

English is increasingly becoming global, and people are increasingly migrating to Anglophone countries, creating an ever increasing need for teaching English for people who don't have adequate knowledge in that language. Leadership skills, which are taken seriously only in career life, are now being taught in schools. As stated by Steven R. Covey in the book "The Leader in Me", started in A.B. Combs Elementary school, Raleigh, North Carolina and spread to other continents of the world, the initiative to teach leadership in schools brought tremendous results in North America, South America, and Asia.

If Leadership skills can be taught to children, why not Standard English? (Actually communication and leadership skills are inseparable.) This book is a genuine attempt to solve the mystery of learning or teaching Standard English. Many people, especially students, are plagued with a dull and uninteresting way of learning English. In addition, they are forced to learn, and most of them hate it. They are struggling to learn and to communicate in English because they are taught English in a complicated way, but this book simplifies English learning. *Where communication problems abound, real progress cannot be made.*

Therefore, I humbly request you to take action to frame policies to teach English this new way—the ice cream way. I believe implementing this method in school or college curriculum will change every fabric of your country to the better—educationally, economically, intellectually, socially, and culturally.

> The presidency is not merely an administrative office . . . It is pre-eminently a place of moral leadership. All our great presidents were leaders of thought at times when certain historic ideas in the life of the nation had to be clarified.
>
> —Franklin D. Roosevelt

> Young people are the drivers of economic development. Foregoing this potential is an economic waste and can undermine social stability. It is important to focus on comprehensive and integrated strategies that combine education and trained policies with targeted employment policies for youth.
>
> —Juan Somavia, Director-General of International Labor Organization

I hope your administration gives this problem (English-learning problem) the attention it deserves.

Most Respectfully
Shalom Kumar Sigworth

Note to the School/College Administrators (teachers)

In the 1980s, I was studying in my first grade (UK English equivalent: first standard) at a school in my home town—Madurai, Tamil Nadu, South India. We were all instructed by our school Principal to speak only English, and not out mother tongue—Tamil. Even though I was a child, I reasoned, "How can I speak English when I do know it?" A person cannot give out what he or she doesn't have in them initially. At that time, I didn't have any English in me nor do my parents or teachers have put in me any English. I was much annoyed by this strict rule prevailing in my school. Worst of all, the school started collecting fines from students speaking Tamil. Many children shut themselves in rather than speak any language. Some of them were secretly talking Tamil in our school. How can communication happen when a person shuts himself rather than try expressing his or her thoughts?

My parents have worked their fingers to the bone to send me to this school so that the teachers would put in me some English and nurture me patiently so that some English will come out. The word "Education" is derived from the latin "educare", which means to "draw out". To bring out something, you need to first put in something. How can you expect an ice cream machine to produce ice creams if you don't first put the ingredients into it? The ice cream manufacturer has to put the milk, egg yolk, sugar, salt, color, flavor, and any other ingredient into the machine so that the machine mix the ingredients, whip them, and bring out the colorful and flavored ice creams to our viewing and tasting pleasure.

The teachers, instead of nurturing, started torturing with their words to bring out something that they have not first put in—English. I'm not writing this to condemn the teachers. I'm compassionate for them because the teachers have been instructed to do so, and they are doing it without realizing the serious damage they are making in the lives of those tender students. Nor do I condemn the school management because they are actually taking the initiative to make their students learn English. The motivation is correct, but the problem lies in the approach to meet the need. My whole idea of writing this book is not to find fault in others, but to help in some way to stop this suffering. As far as I know, this madness did not stop in my school. I guess this madness may still be continuing in many other parts of the globe.

> What do we live for if it is not to make life less difficult to each other.
>
> —George Eliot

> If I can stop one heart from breaking,
> I shall not live in vain;
> If I can ease one life the aching,
> Or cool one pain,
> Or help one fainting robin
> Unto his nest again,
> I shall not live in vain.
>
> —Emily Dickinson

The following facts taken from the article "English-Only Instruction at Korean Universities: Help or Hindrance to higher learning" by Hyun-Sook Kang, published in the journal *English Today* (vol. 28, no. 1, March 2012) would help you understand the seriousness of the issue—English learning by non-English speakers. Recently, few students at one of South Korea's prestigious universities committed suicide, and partial blame went to the new institutional policy (English-only instruction) enforced by the university's top administrator. (The incidence was originally published in The New York Times on 22 May 2011, with the title 'Elite South Korean University rattled by suicides'.)

The general prevailing attitude concerning English-only instruction is: If students are allowed to interact in their native language, English learning will be hampered. (Note: In French-learning institutes, speaking in English is not at all allowed; French is taught using French not using English.) But according to study by August and Shannan, the use of native tongue facilitated second language acquisition and literacy development. Research conducted for UNESCO in 2008 found that in 26 countries, the language of instruction was linked to more than 50% of school dropout among children who did not speak the school language (English).

Just because they are taught through English does not mean that children will automatically learn English. A sudden shift to English-only instruction (UK English: English-medium instruction) without the proper teaching of the native language will lead to educational failure. Many of the students have failed to have the employable skills the employers are looking for because there has been a mismatch between what the industries want and what the schools and colleges are producing.

> Current systems of education were not designed to meet the challenges we now face. They were developed to meet the needs of a former age. Reform is not enough: they need to be transformed.
>
> —Ken Robinson, *Out of Our Minds:*
> *Learning to be Creative*

SUSTAINED EDUCATION IN MOTHER TONGUE AND THE DEVELOPMENT OF MOTHER TONGUE ARE EQUALLY IMPORTANT. The following quote emphasizes this point:

> As regards the vernaculars, which must for long be the sole instrument for the diffusion of knowledge among all except a small minority of Indian People, we found them in danger of being neglected and degraded in pursuit of English, and in many cases very bad English, for the sake of mercantile value. By all means let English be taught to those who are qualified to learn it; but let it rest upon a solid foundation of the indigenous languages, for NO PEOPLE WILL EVER USE ANOTHER TONGUE WITH ADVANTAGE THAT CANNOT FIRST USE ITS OWN WITH EASE
> —Lord Curzon [*Emphasis Added*]

I'm a living example of a person who learnt English effectively via my mother tongue Tamil, in a private English-coaching institute, and out of my own willingness to learn and not out of compulsion. Every country's native language and culture is unique and they should be appreciated and respected. What happens if there is only one ice cream and that there is only one flavor of ice cream? This leads to Ice cream eating becoming a boring task. Ice cream eating is still the most enjoyable experience because of the availability of a huge variety of flavors. It is the variety that attracts us. Similarly, it is the diversity of language and culture of every nation is what makes this world beautiful and fascinating. So please stop the madness of torturing the children with "speak-only-English" instruction in schools.

Engage your children in native tongue sufficiently, and slowly but subtly introduce English.

> We think all children should at least begin their schooling in their mother tongue, and that they will benefit from being taught in their mother tongue as long as possible.
>
> —UNESCO, 1951

If you can autonomously choose your curriculum, please test this ice cream method in your schools or colleges and, upon finding the method satisfactory, implement them in your school or college curriculum. If you cannot do this without the consent of the Ministry of Education in your country, please take steps to persuade your Education minister to frame policies to implement this new method, and later on, implement the same in your institutions.

> Don't try to fix the students; fix ourselves first. The good teacher makes the poor student good, and the good student superior. When our students fail, we as teachers, too, have failed.
>
> —Marva Collins

> The research is clear: nothing motivates a child more than when learning is valued by schools and families/ communities working together in partnership ... Those forms of involvement do not happen by accident or even by invitation. They happen by explicit strategic intervention.
>
> —Michael Fullan

In the world of education, there is no lack of creativity, passion, caring, or research as to how to create a great school, a great classroom, or a great student. More often than not, the great barrier to success is that the systems and processes are not in place to sustain excellence.

—Stephen Covey

Never doubt that a small group of thoughtful, committed citizens can change the world. Indeed, it is the only thing ever has.

—Margaret Mead

Note to Parents

Dear Parents

Give your child a head start in English learning. The use of English as a world language for Aviation, Information technology, Science and Teaching, and the expansion of European Union are increasingly making English the international language. Your child need not have to wait for decades to learn Standard English, which is practiced in all careful writing. Anybody with a basic ability to read and understand English can easily use this book and understand the concepts it explains.

If you are serious about your child's English learning, this book can be of a great help. Armed with this book, you can influence your child's English acquisition within the four walls of your house, as you are your child's first teacher—the best teacher!

> Home—A centre of love and affection—is the best place for education and first school of a child.
>
> —Pestalozzi

All the basics of grammar, syntax, punctuation, the four modules of communication (reading, writing, listening, and speaking), and practical communication problems are addressed in detail in this book. You need not have to cram all the grammar into your child's brain. The book is written to make grammar easy and fun. Most of all, grammar is divided in the form of 40 ice creams and 103 licks. All you have to do is give your child one ice cream a day or rather one lick of an ice cream a day. You can give actual ice creams to lure your child into learning grammar. You can use a lot of fruit extract and change it to ice creams. This way your child's nutrition, along with grammar learning, is also taken care of in an intelligent and interesting way.

You need not have to do one more thing along with many other things you do for your child. If you could do just one thing—teach your child just one aspect a day—is sufficient. A LITTLE ADDED EVERY DAY to your child's learning for some months or years will surely give you a compounding interest on your investment in your child's education.

> If I were asked what single qualification was necessary for one who has the care of children, I should say patience. Patience with their tempers, with their understandings, with their progress. Patience to go over first principles again and again, steadily TO ADD A LITTLE EVERY DAY.
>
> —Fenelon [*Emphasis added*]

> Patience, endless patience . . . OUR CHILDREN BECOME WHAT WE PAY ATTENTION TO.
>
> —R. Hill [*Emphasis added*]

So relax, have peace of mind, and religiously follow the "TEACH GRAMMAR ONE AT A TIME" prescription given in this book. You need not have to sweat too much. Just add a little each day. I hope that, by learning English this ice cream way, your child will become an excellent communicator—an excellent orator or a prolific writer or a great leader in his/her chosen field.

> The best thing about the future is that it comes only ONE DAY AT A TIME.
>
> —Abraham Lincoln [*Emphasis added*]

APPENDIX II.
RESOURCES TO STUDENTS

Note to students

Dear Student

Are you working like hell and not taking time to enjoy life? Or, are you drifting through life, living aimless, just coasting your time, and not giving enough thought to your after-school or after-college life? Having fun is not at all wrong. But having only fun and not working at all is the problem of some people. On the far end, involving only in work and not having enough fun is the problem of some other people. A balance of little seriousness and little fun is needed for everyone. You need to work and equally, you need to play.

> All work and no play makes Jack a dull boy; but all play and no work makes him something greatly worse.
> —Samuel Smiles

So amidst of your tight schedules of academic life, friends, family engagements, and your dreams and efforts, you can wisely spend some 30 minutes to an hour for your English learning every day for about just 5–6 months. To achieve your goal, you must start somewhere; otherwise, you cannot achieve your goals.

> Start is what stops many people.
> —Don Shula

If you want to have a great life, mastering English is the key. So if you are yearning for a great life, why not start learning today? Why not start right now?

> Adopt a "do-it-now" attitude because NOW is the time to succeed.
>> —Nikita Koloff & Jeffrey Gitomer,
>> *Wrestling with Success*

The wisdom for easy, enjoyable, and memorable way to learn English is to LEARN ONE THING AT A TIME (see the study plan given in the following section). If you take any activity in life, it is a process. Everything from doing laundry to becoming a professional is a process taking ONE STEP AT A TIME. You cannot just heap a load of bricks and declare that your house is built. You cannot just keep kicking goals in your opponents' goal post in the field of football. This can happen only if you play all by yourself and without any opponents. Playing in the real field is difficult—you need to pass the ball, tackle the opponents' moves, and need to communicate and cooperate with your fellow players before scoring a goal.

> A house is built ONE BRICK AT A TIME. Football games are won A PLAY AT A TIME. Every big accomplishment is a series of little accomplishments.
>> —David J. Schwartz, *The Magic of Thinking Big*
>> [*Emphasis added*]

> My intention being to acquire the habitude of all these virtues, I judged it would be well not to distract my

attention by attempting the whole at once, but to fix
ONE OF THEM AT A TIME.

> —Benjamin Franklin, in describing his desire
> to possess thirteen virtues, in his autobiography
> [*Emphasis added*]

The shortest way to do many things is to ONLY DO
ONE THING AT ONCE.

> —Samuel Smiles [*Emphasis added*]

It is a mistake to try to look too far ahead. The chain
of destiny can only be grasped ONE LINK AT A TIME.

> —Winston Churchill

It is the presence of opposition or barriers is what makes
playing a game interesting (not the absence of barriers), and
what makes winning the trophy worthwhile and glorious.
The same is the process of mastering English. Keep your eyes
on your objective, and the obstacles must give way.

> We are built to conquer environment, solve problems,
> achieve goals, and we find no real satisfaction or
> happiness in life without obstacles to conquer and
> goals to achieve.
>
> —Maxwell Maltz

> Change will not come if we wait for some other
> person or some other time. We are the ones we've
> been waiting for. We are the change that we seek.
>
> —Barack Obama

I set out to change the world but quickly realized I couldn't. So I decided to change my nation but realized I couldn't do that either. So I decided to change my city. When that didn't happen I thought, I'll just change my family. But that didn't happen either. And then it hit me why don't I just change myself? And when I did, it changed my family, my city, my nation, and my world.

—Engravings on a gravestone in England.

Study Plan (Action Plan)

> Success consists of a series of little daily victories.
> —Laddie F. Hutar

> The easiest way to implement the pre-determined outcome formula is to divide your desired achievements into small daily amounts. The "daily dose" is the rocket ship. Your achievement actions are the fuel.
> —Nikita Koloff & Jeffrey Gitomer,
> *Wrestling with Success*

Dear reader

A written document regarding any activity helps you to do that activity at a much higher precision and in less time than when you don't have one. The following is the study plan (action plan) to show you how learning a little each day (just like licking an ice cream each moment) can add up to your education. All you have to do is A LITTLE LEARNING ONE STEP AT A TIME. Remember: *A lot of little streams make up an ocean.*

For each day, you will be given a grammar aspect you need to learn. In addition, for each day, you will be given a thought-provoking quotation to motivate you, to think about real issues, and most importantly to engage you in action—action that will make you to TREAD grammar not DREAD it. After you finish learning one aspect, you have to tick the box given in the study plan. This way you can see your progress without having anybody to supervise you. You were also given enough blank lines to write your precious thoughts related to the grammar learning. Good luck in your learning!

A good plan is like a road map: it shows the final destination and usually the best way to get there.

—H. Stanley Judd

Whatever course you decide upon, there is always someone to tell you that you are wrong. There are always difficulties arising which tempt you to believe that your critics are right. To map out a course of action and follow it to an end requires courage.

—Ralph Waldo Emerson

DAY 1

NOUNS ☐

Do not wait. The time will never be just right. Start where you stand.... – Napoleon Hill

---

Day 2

Proper and common nouns ☐

Even a high tower starts on the ground.— Japanese Proverb

Day 3

Concrete and abstract nouns ☐

He who has begun, has the work half done.— Horace

Day 4

Collective and mass nouns ☐

Don't waste time waiting for inspiration. Begin and inspiration will find you.—Thomas Edison

---

Day 5

Function of nouns ☐

Your progress in life begins in your mind and ends in the same place.—Napolean Hill –

Day 6

PRONOUNS ☐

Whether you believe you can do a thing or not, you are right.—Henry Ford

Day 7

Personal
pronouns ☐

...Our faith beforehand in an uncertifiable result is the only thing that makes the result come true.— William James

Day 8

Demonstrative
pronouns ☐

For those who believe, no proof is necessary....—John & Lyn St. Clair Thomas

Day 9

Relative
pronouns ☐

The master key to success lies in your capacity to believe that you will succeed.—Napoleon Hill

Day 10

Interrogative
pronouns ☐

...A decline in courage has been considered the beginning of the end.—Solzhenitsyn

Day 11

Indefinite
pronouns ☐

Everything comes down to courage at the sticking point.—Margaret Thatcher

Day 12

Reflexive
pronouns ☐

...It is because we do not dare that things are difficult.—Seneca

Day 13

VERBS ☐ - - - - - - - - - - - - - - -

The key to everything is patience.... —Arnold Glasgow

Day 14

Function of verbs ☐

Patience, the essential quality of a man. —Kwai-Koo-Tsu

Day 15

Types of verbs ☐ - - -

Nothing in the world can take the place of persistence... —Calvin Coolidge

Day 16

Variation of verbs ☐

...My strength solely lies in my tenacity. —Louis Pasteur

Day 17

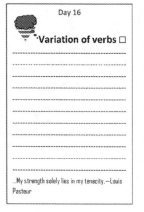

ADJECTIVES ☐ - - - - - - - - - -

The only difference between the big shot and the little shot is that the big shot was simply the little shot that kept on shooting. —Zig Ziglar

Day 18

Position of adjectives ☐ - - - - - - - - - - - - - - -

To achieve what you want, you must want enough to achieve —Walter M. Germain

Day 19

Number of adjectives ☐-------------------

The greatest things ever done on Earth have been done little by little. —William Jennings Bryan

Day 20

Degrees of comparison ☐-------------------

Work joyfully and peacefully, knowing that right thoughts and right efforts inevitably bring about right results. —James Allen

Day 21

Adverbs ☐-------------------

We write our destiny. We become what we do. —Madame Chiang Kai-Shek

Day 22

Confusion with adjectives ☐-------------------

The biggest risk we all face is not moving forward with what we've learned. —Donald Trump

Day 23

Positioning of adverbs ☐-------------------

If you want your dreams come true, don't sleep, act! —Yiddish Proverb

Day 24

Articles ☐-------------------

...You have to succeed in doing what is necessary. —Winston Churchill

Day 25

Choosing the right article ☐-----------------------

...The way to success is organized thinking followed by action! action! action!---Napoleon Hill

Day 26

Functions of articles ☐-----------------------

I dream my painting, and then I paint my dream.---Vincent van Gogh

Day 27

Conjunctions ☐-----

The world pins no medal on you because of what you know, but it may crown you with glory and riches for what you do.---Napoleon Hill

Day 28

Types of conjunctions ☐-----------------

Stride forward with a firm, steady step knowing...that you will achieve every aim.-- Eileen Caddy

Day 29

Subordinating conjunctions ☐-----------------

Spectacular performance is always preceded by unspectacular preparation.--Robert Schuller

Day 30

Coordinating conjunction vs. coordinating adverb ☐-----

What you do now creates your future.--Dr. Joe Vitale

Day 31

Preposition ☐-----

...The secret of your success is found in your daily routine.—John C. Maxwell

Day 32

Syntax in prepositional phrases ☐----

Let the motive for the action be in the action itself.—Bhagavad Gita

Day 33

Unnecessary repetition of prepositions ☐----

Can anything be sadder than work left unfinished? Yes, work never begun.—Christina Rossetti

Day 34

Case of pronoun to be followed ☐----

You cannot control the wind. But you can control your sails.—Tonny Robins

Day 35

Misuse of preposition ☐----

Keep going and the chances are you will stumble on something...—Charles Kettering

Day 36

You shall not end a sentence with Preposition ☐----

Not only strike while the iron is hot, but make it hot by striking.—Oliver Cromwell

Day 37

Interjections ☐----

Challenges are what makes life interesting; overcoming them is what makes life meaningful.—Joshua J. Marine

Day 38

Phrases ☐-------

People begin to become successful the minute they decide to be.—Harvey Mackay

Day 39

Prepositional phrases ☐-------

He who is not everyday conquering some fear has not learned the secret of the life.—Ralph Waldo Emerson

Day 40

Punctuation in prepositional phrases ☐----

We grow because we struggle. we learn and we overcome—R.C. Allen

Day 41

Infinitive phrases ☐

Every day you make progress. Every step may be fruitful.—Winston Churchill

Day 42

Split infinitives ☐--

When a man no longer possesses a motive for living and no future to look toward, he curls up in a corner and dies.—Victor Frankl

Day 43

Participial phrases ☐

What we love to do we find time to do. —Jean Lancaster Spaulding

Day 44

Dangling modifier ☐

Right now is the most important moment in your life. —Robert Fritz

Day 45

Dangling participles ☐

Whatever you do, do it with intelligence, and keep the end in view. —Thomas à Kempis

Day 46

Present and past participles ☐

Whenever I hear it can't be done, I know I'm close to success. —Mary Kay Ash

Day 47

Gerund phrases ☐

...Belief is the ignition switch that gets you off the launching pad. —Dennis Waitley

Day 48

Clauses ☐

Ability is what gives you the opportunity; belief is what gets you there. —Apollo

Day 49

Independent clauses ☐------------------------------

The only place where your dream becomes impossible is in your own thinking.—Robert Schuller

Day 50

Punctuating independent clauses ☐-----

We all have the extraordinary coded inside us, waiting to be released.—Jean Houston

Day 51

Dependent clauses ☐------------------------------

If you hear a voice within you say 'you cannot paint,' by all the means paint and that voice will be silenced.—Vincent Van Gogh

Day 52

That vs. which ☐

You are the one who can stretch your horizon.—Edgar Magnin

Day 53

Sentences ☐---------

Give your dreams all you got and you'll be amazed at the energy that comes out of you.—William James

Day 54

Questions ☐---------

Motivation is what gets you started. Habit is what keeps you going.—Unknown

Day 55

Exclamations ☐------

The best way to predict the future is to create it.—Unknown

Day 56

Simple sentences ☐

Picture in your mind a sense of personal destiny.—Wayne Oates

Day 57

Concepts in simple sentences ☐----------

You got to get up every morning with determination if you're going to bed with satisfaction.—George Horace Lorimer

Day 58

Compound sentences ☐----------

Never fear the space between your dreams and reality. If you can dream it, you can make it so.—Belva Davis

Day 59

Punctuating compound sentences ☐--

I believe that when you realize who you really are, you understand that nothing can stop you from becoming that person.—Christine Lincoln

Day 60

The comma splice ☐

If we did all the things we are capable of, we would literally astound ourselves.—Thomas Edison

Day 61

Complex sentences ☐ ----------

I don't ever look back. I look forward. —Steffi Graf

Day 62

Compound–complex sentences ☐ -------

I'm a slow walker, but I never walk back.— Abraham Lincoln

Day 63

Length of sentences ☐ ----------

By striving we reach the stars. —Royal Air Force Motto

Day 64

PARAGRAPHS ☐ ---

Wheresoever you go, go with all the heart.— Confucius

Day 65

Structure of a paragraph ☐ ----------

...Today well lived makes every yesterday a dream of happiness and every tomorrow a vision of hope.—Unknown

Day 66

Length of a paragraph ☐ ----------

It's okay to make mistakes. Mistakes are our teachers—they help us to learn.—John Bradshaw

Day 67

Example of a well-written paragraph ☐

Why do we fall? So we can pick up ourselves.—
The movie "Batman begins"

Day 68

CHANGE IN VERBS (Tense, voice, mood) ☐----

Heroism consist in hanging on one minute longer.—Norwegian Proverb

Day 69

Tense ☐-------------

Our grand business is not to see what lies dimly in the distance, but to do what lies clearly at hand.—Thomas Carlyle

Day 70

Present tense ☐

First ponder, then dare.—Helmuth Moltke

Day 71

Past tense ☐

Today's preparation determines tomorrow's achievement.—Thomas Edison

Day 72

Future tense ☐

A man can succeed at almost anything for which he has unlimited enthusiasm.—Charles M. Schwab

Day 73

Present perfect tense ☐--------------------------

Enthusiasm and persistence can make an average person superior.—William Ward

Day 74

Past perfect tense ☐--------------------------

If you aren't fired with enthusiasm, you will be fired with enthusiasm.—Vince Lombardi

Day 75

Future perfect tense ☐--------------------------

I only see the objective...the obstacle must give way.—Napoleon Bonaparte

Day 76

- Progressive tenses ☐--------------------------

The goal becomes both the target and the fuel.—Denis Waitley

Day 77

Shift in tenses ☐--

Light tomorrow with today.—Elizabeth Barrett Browning

Day 78

VOICE ☐--------------------------

Enthusiasm is a disease, it spreads.—David Goh

Day 79

- Forming the Passive voice □ --------------

You can learn new things at any time in your life if you're willing to be a beginner. If you actually learn to like being a beginner, the whole world opens up to you.—Barbara Sher

Day 80

Improper & proper use of passive voice □ ------

By failing to prepare you are preparing to fail.—Benjamin Franklin

Day 81

MOOD □

Our goals can only be reached through the vehicle of a plan, in which we must fervently believe, upon which we must vigorously act. There is no other route to success.—Stephen A. Brennan

Day 82

Indicative mood □

View mistakes as missed takes—take mistakes and learn their relevance.—Brad Turk

Day 83

Imperative mood □

Set your goals high, and don't stop till you get there.—Bo Jackson

Day 84

Subjunctive mood □

You have to have faith and believe in yourself.—Gail Devers

Day 85

PUNCTUATION ☐

To make a great dream come true, you must first have a great dream. —Dr. Hans Salye

Day 86

Periods ☐

Believe that you have it, and you have it. —Latin Proverb

Day 87

Ending a sentence ☐

One skill that you act on is better than twelve that you don't. —Brad Turk

Day 88

After Initials/abbreviations ☐

Do your thing and I shall know you. —Ralph Waldo Emerson

Day 89

QUESTION MARKS ☐

Action may not always bring happiness, but there is no happiness without action. —William James

Day 90

EXCLAMATIONS ☐

Kites rise highest against the wind—not with it. —Winston Churchill

---

Day 91

Indicating surprise, humor, joy ☐

Faith is the ability to see the INVISIBLE, believe in the INCREDIBLE, in order to receive what the masses think is IMPOSSIBLE. — Clarence Smithison [Emphasis added]

Day 92

Indicating fear, anger, pain, or danger ☐

Destroy fear through action. —David Schwartz, *The Magic of Thinking Big*

Day 93

Giving orders ☐

Whether you believe you can do a thing or not, you are right.—Henry Ford

---

Day 94

Parentheses ☐

You have removed most of the road block to success when you've learned the difference between motion and direction.—Bill Copeland

---

Day 95

Brackets ☐

We are what we think. All that we are arises with our thoughts. With our thoughts we make our world.—Buddha

---

Day 96

Indicating alteration or annotation ☐

The ability to focus attention on important things is a defining characteristic of intelligence.—Robert Schiller

Day 97

Giving additional information to another extra information ☐----------

It is a mark of intelligence, no matter what you are doing, to have a good time doing it.— Unknown

Day 98

APOSTROPHES ☐

The moment you say 'I give up' someone else seeing the same situation is saying 'my, what an opportunity'. -- Benjamin Franklin

Day 99

Possession of Singular nouns ☐----------------

The ultimate measure of a man is not where he stands in moments of comfort and convenience, but where he stands in times of challenge.— Martin Luther King

Day 100

Plural nouns ending in "s" ☐----------------

When you are committed to something, you accept no excuses, only results.—Kenneth Blanchard

Day 101

Plural nouns not ending in "s" ☐----------------

...Your own resolution to succeed is more important...—Abraham Lincoln

Day 102

Persons whose Names ending in "s" ☐-----

Strive for perfection but settle for excellence.— Henry Ford

Day 103

Omitting letters ☐

Your circumstances may be uncongenial, but they shall not remain so if you perceive an ideal and strive to reach it. --James Allen

DAY 104

Omitting numbers ☐

Indeed one's faith in one's plans and methods are truly tested when the horizon before one is the blackest. --Mahatma Gandhi

DAY 105

SLASH ☐

I always know the ending; that's where I start-- Toni Morrison

DAY 106

HYPHEN ☐

When you cannot make up your mind which of two evenly balanced courses of action you should take--choose the bolder. --W.J. Slim

DAY 107

Forming compound nouns and compound adjectives ☐

For the purposes of action nothing is more useful than narrowness of thought combined with energy of will. --Henri Frederic Amiel

DAY 108

Noun + participle, or adjective + participle ☐

Success seems to be connected with action. Successful men keep moving. They make mistakes, but they don't quit. --Conrad Hilton

DAY 109

Forming group of words ☐----------------------

Nothing ventured, nothing gained. —Proverb

DAY 110

Special compound words ☐----------

To do nothing is the way to be nothing. —Nathiel Howe

DAY 111

Numbers and fractions ☐----------------

A life spent making mistakes is not only more honorable but more useful than a life spent doing nothing. — George Bernrad Shaw

DAY 112

Avoiding confusion of compound words ☐----------------------

Act boldly and unseen forces will come to your aid. — Dorotha Brande

DAY 113

Normal word vs. prefix word ☐--------------------

Success is a matter of understanding and religiously practicing specific, simple habits that always lead to success.— Robert J. Ringer

DAY 114

Avoiding succession of same letters ☐--------------

The man who succeeds has a program. He fixes his course and adheres to it. He lays his plans and executes them.—Unknown

DAY 115

QUOTATION MARKS □----------------------

Seize the day!--Horace

DAY 116

Indicating Direct quotations □-----------------

Take one giant step at a time.....--John Maxwell

DAY 117

Quotation within a main quotation □----------

Don't let your learning lead to knowledge: let your learning lead to action--Jim Rohn

DAY 118

Long quotations □

Start by doing what's necessary, then what's possible and suddenly you are doing the impossible.--Francis of Assisi

DAY 119

Position of punctuation marks □--------

Just try to do something--just being there, showing up--is how we get braver. Self-esteem is about doing. -- Joy Browned

DAY 120

COMMA □--------

All the beautiful sentiments in the world weigh less than a simple lovely action.--James Russell Lowell

DAY 121

Serial comma ☐

Do it now...and before anyone tells you to do it!—Napoleon Hill

DAY 122

Setting off interruptions ☐----------------

If you can dream it, you can do it. Always remember that this whole thing was started with a dream and a mouse.—Walt Disney

DAY 123

After Introductory words ☐------

The world cares very little about what a man or woman knows; it is what a man or woman is able to do that counts.—Booker T. Washington

DAY 124

Between two unrelated sentences ☐-----

Life is trying things to see if they work.—Ray Brandbury

DAY 125

After coordinating adverbs ☐----

...The greatest failure is to not try.—Debbi Fields

DAY 126

Single vs. double commas ☐--------------

Why not spend some time in determining what is worthwhile...then go after that?—William Ross

DAY 127

COLON ☐--------

You must draw on language, logic and simple common sense to determine essential issues and establish a concrete course of action.—Abraham Lincoln

---

DAY 128

Introducing a speech or quotation ☐-----

How you do what you do will determine who you will become.—Bob Livingston

---

DAY 129

Introducing a list ☐--------

Unless you try to do something beyond what you have already mastered, you will never grow.—Ralph Waldo Emerson

---

DAY 130

Introducing a summary ☐----------------

It is difficult to lay aside a confirmed passion.—Caius Valerius Catullus

---

DAY 131

Introducing amplification or illustration ☐--------

If you cannot excel with talent, then triumph with effort.—Dave Weinbaum

---

DAY 132

Colon vs. semicolon ☐--------

Either you step forward into growth or you will step back into safety.—Abraham Maslow

DAY 133

SEMICOLON ☐

It has been my observation that most people get ahead during the time that others waste.—Henry Ford

DAY 134

Between two independent classes ☐

I never did a day's work in my life, it was all fun.—Edison

DAY 135

Connecting an Ind. clause + coord. adverb and another Ind. clause ☐

If one advances confidently in the direction of his dreams...he will meet with a success unexpected in common hours.—Henry David Thoreau

DAY 136

Breaking up of a list ☐

Nothing splendid has ever been achieved except by those who dared believe that something inside them was superior to their circumstance.—Bruce Barton

DAY 137

Semicolon vs. period ☐

When the wind of changes blow, some build wind protection, others build windmills.—Mao Tse-tung

DAY 138

Dashes ☐

Concentrate all your thoughts upon the work at hand. The sun rays do not burn until brought to a focus.—Alexander Graham Bell

DAY 139

Announcing an appositive or summary ☐

It is not the will to win, but the will to prepare to win that makes the difference.—Paul "Bear" Bryant

DAY 140

Indicating a contrast or surprise ☐-----

The winner is he who gives himself to work, body and soul.—Charles Buxton

DAY 141

Making an emphasis ☐----------------------

Winning isn't the important thing. It is the only thing.--George Allen

DAY 142

Setting off breaks in thought ☐----------

When you win...you won't remember the pain.—Joe Namath

DAY 143

Avoid using more dashes in a sentence ☐-----

Winning breeds confidence and confidence breeds winning.—Hubert Green

BIBLIOGRAPHY

P. Gayler. Paul Gayler's Little Book of Ice Creams & Sorbets: Sumptuous, Mouth-Watering, Refreshing. Kyle Cathie Ltd.: London.

The Hindu. Naturally, Yours. La Cream Boast Exotic Varieties of Ice Creams Made with Fruit Extracts. Saturday, 21 Dec 2013.

M. Fitzgerald. 2013. Why Do We Get "Ice Cream Headaches" and How Can We Avoid Them? http://blog. positscience.com/2013/08/19/why-do-we-get-ice-cream-headaches-and-how-can-we-avoid-them/

Ice Cream Head Ache. http://en.wikipedia.org/wiki/Brain_freeze

D. Rowles. Why Does Eating Ice Cream Make You Thirsty? June 20, 2013. http://www.pajiba.com/miscellaneous/why-does-eating-ice-cream-make-you-thirsty.php#.Uqk7DdIW3aY

http://curiosity.discovery.com/question/why-there-salt-ice-cream

English

Robert A. Day. 2000. Scientific English: A Guide for Scientists and Other Professionals, 2nd edn. Universities Press: Hyderabad, India.

J.L. Kinneavy & J.E. Warriner. Elements of Writing, 4th course. HBJ: Fort Worth, TX.

W. Strunk & E.B. White. 2000. The Elements of Style, 4th edn. Longman: New York.

C.L. Wrenn. The English Language. AITBS publishers: New Delhi.

P. Sebranek, D. Kemper & V. Meyer. 1999. WRITE SOURCE 2000: A Guide to Writing, Thinking, and Learning. Houghton Mifflin: Wilmington, MA.

C. Goodwright & J. Olearski. 2009. In the English-Speaking World. Chancerel: London.

http://www.theguardian.com/education/2012/nov/13/confusing-tesol-training

http://www.nuffieldfoundation.org/barriers-bangladeshis-learning-or-improving-english

http://www.nuffieldfoundation.org/barriers-bangladeshis-learning-or-improving-english

H. Li, R.F. Fox, D.J. 2007. Almarza. Strangers in Stranger Lands: Language, Learning, Culture. *International Journal of Progressive Education* 3 (1).

M.A. Webb, D. Stewart, L. Bunting, & H. Regan. January 2012. Breaking Down Barriers to Learning: Primary School-Based Learning. No. 14 Policy and Practice Briefing. Barnardo's Northern Ireland: Belfast, UK. www.barnardos.org.uk

NEET National Research Project. Motivation and Barriers to Learning for Young People not in Education, Employment or

Training. Feb 2013. BIS Research Paper No. 87. Department of Business, Innovation and skills: London. http://www.gov.uk/government/organisations/department-for-business-innovation skills/

B. Hedges. 2012. Read and Get Rich: How the Hidden Power of Reading Can Make you Rich in all Areas of your Life. Pentagon Press: New Delhi, India.

M. Nurnberg & M. Rosenblum. 1995. All About Words: An Adult Approach to Vocabulary Building. Goyl Saab publishers: New Delhi.

G. King. 2005. Collins Good Writing Guide. HaperCollins: Glasgow, UK.

A.S. Hornby. 2005. Oxford Advanced Learner's Dictionary, 7th edn. Oxford University Press: Oxford, UK.

R. Gee & C. Watson. 2003. The Usborne Guide to Better English: Grammar, Spelling and Punctuation. Usborne: London.

R.L. Trask. 2001. Mind the Gaffe: The Penguin Guide to Common Errors in English. Penguin: New Delhi.

A.N. Applebee et al. 2000. The Language of Literature: American Literature. McDougal Littell: Evanston, IL.

J. Adair. 1997. Effective Communication: The Most Important Management Tool of All. Pan Books: London.

P. Ahuja & J.C. Ahuja. 1991. Learning to Read Effectively and Efficiently. Sterling publishers: New Delhi.

David Graddol. 2010. English Next. British Council: UK.

J. Peat, E. Elliott, L. Baur, & V. Keena. 2002. Scientific Writing: Easy when you know how. BMJ books: London.

H.-S. Kang. March 2012. English-Only Instruction at Korean Universities: Help or Hindrance to higher learning. *English Today* 28 (1): 29–34.

D. August & T. Shannon. 2006. Developing Literacy in Second-language learners: Report of the National Literacy Panel on Language-minority Children and Youth. Laurence Erlbaum Associates: Mahwah, NJ.

N. Krishnaswamy & L. Krishnaswamy. The Story of English in India. 2006. Foundation Books: New Delhi.

E. Bird and M. Dennison. 1987. Teaching GCSE Modern Languages. Hodder and Stoughton: London, UK.

S. Griffith. 1997. Teaching English Abroad: Talk Your Way around the World. Vacation Work: Oxford, UK.

General

S.R. Covey. 2008. The Leader in Me: How Schools and Parents around the World are Inspiring Greatness, One Child at a Time. Simon & Schuster: London.

M. Hauge. 1991. Writing Screenplays that Sell: The Complete, Step-By-Step Guide for Writing and Selling to the Movies and TV, from the Story Concept to Development Deal. Harpercollins: New York.

D. Agarwal. 2004. My Book of Creative Writing. Scholastic: New Delhi.

P. Baker. Secrets of Super Achievers. 2004. Lion Book: Oxford, UK.

J.S. Hill. World Business. 2005. Thomson–South-western: Ohio.

N. Hill & J. Williamson. 2010. 52 Lessons for Life: A Quote a Week to Change Your Life. Collins Business: Noida, India.

D. Trump & R. Kiyosaki. 2007. Why We Want You to be Rich: Two Men, One Message. Rich Press

R. Kiyosaki & S. Lechter. 2001. Rich Kid Smart Kid: Giving your Child a Financial Head Start. Warner Books: New York.

http://www.gov.uk/government/organisations/department-for-business-innovation skills/

D. Kimbro & N. Hill. 1991. Think and Grow Rich: A Black Choice. Fawcett Books: New York.

S. Covey. 2006. The 6 Most Important Decisions you'll Ever Make: A Guide for Teens. Simon & Schuster: New York.

Gerry Robert. The Millionaire Mindset: How Ordinary People Can Create Extraordinary Income. Lifesuccess Publishing: Scottsdale, AZ

R.H. Schuller. 1983. Tough Times Never Last, but Tough People Do! Bantam Books: New York.

Ultimate Visual Dictionary: 21st Century Supplement. Dorling Kindersley: London. ISBN: 0-1430-3012-4.

S.K. Sigworth. 2013. Why Do We Need Teachers? http://mindtomanifest.blogspot.com

J. Hinshaw et al. 2006. Volume Library 2: A Modern Authoritative Reference for Home and School Use. Southwestern: Nashville, TN

Vanaja & Vanaja Bharathi. Value-Oriented Education: Initiatives at the Teacher-Education Level. 2008. Neelkamal: New Delhi.

Harold & Sandy Moe. 1987. Teach Your Child The Value of Money: A Proven Success Guide to Help Parents Motivate Children into Successful Futures. Harsand Financial Press: Wisconsin.

C.C. Taylor. 2010. 8 Attributes of Great Achievers. Embassay Books: Mumbai.

Video Visits CANADA. Diskovery Video & Laser Co. Pvt. Ltd.

Times Music. 2008. Travel Guide SINGAPORE. Times Music: Mumbai.

N. Sundarrajan. 2003. Pearls of Wisdom from Personalities Galore. Sura Books: Chennai.

Writing Magazine. March 2014. Warners Group Publications: Leeds, UK. http://www.writers-online.co.uk

D. Booher. 2007. The Voice of Authority: 10 Communication Strategies Every Leader Needs to Know. Tata McGraw Hill: New Delhi.

B.S. Warrier. 2012. Studying Abroad: All You Wanted to Know. Tata McGraw Hill: New Delhi.

C. McCrudden, A. Bourne, & C. Lyons. 2010. You Unlimited. Westland Ltd.

D. Goh. 2006. Blueprint for Greater Success. Sterling Publishers: New Delhi.

J.L. Valentine. 2009. The Man of Power: Ultimate Male Empowerment. JAICO: Mumbai.

D. Quayle. 1999. Worth Fighting for. Word Publishing: Nashville, TN. ISBN: 0-8499-1606-2.

P. Harrington. The Secret to Teen Power. 2009. Simon & Schuster: New York.

J. Caruso. The Power of Losing Control: Finding Strength, Meaning, and Happiness in an Out-of-Control World. Gotham Books: New York.

J.C. Maxwell. 2003. Success One Day at a Time. Magna Books: Mumbai.

B. Zilbergeld, A.A. Lazarus. 1987. Mind Power: Getting What You Want through Mental Training. Ivy Books: New York.

R. Sharma. 2003. Mega Living. JAICO: Mumbai.

J. Vitale. 2006. Life's Missing Instruction Manual: The Guidebook You Should Have Been Given at Birth, Wiley India: New Delhi.

B. Tracy. 2009. Flight Plan. Tata McGraw Hill: New Delhi.

K. Kiyosaki. 2006. Rich Woman: A Book on Investing for Women. Rich Press.

J.D. Murphy. 2003. Why Not You? A Positive Program for Achievement. New Century Book House: Chennai

B. Livingston. How You Do…What You Do. 2008. McGraw Hill: New York. ISBN: 978-0-07-159278-9

C. Barrow, P. Barrow, & R. Brown. 1998. The Business Plan Workbook, 6th edn. Kogan Page: London.

R. Abrams. 2003. The Successful Business Plan Secrets & Strategies, 4th edn. PHI Learning: New Delhi

S.D. Anthony. 2009. The Silver Lining: An Innovation Playbook for Uncertain Times. Harvard Business Review Press: Boston, MA

M. Jensen. 2001. The Everything Business Planning Book: How to Plan for Success in a New or Growing Business. Adams Media Corporation: Fairfield, OH.

T. Ahern & S. Joyaux. 2008. Keep Your Donors: The Guide to Better Communications and Stronger Relationships. Wiley: Hoeboeken, NJ.

S. Hougaard. 2004. The Business Idea: The Early Stages of Entreprenuership. Springer: Hidelberg, Germany

A. Cohen. 2006. Relax into Wealth: How to get more by doing less. Piatkus Books: London.

R. Holden. 2005. Authentic Success: Essential Lessons and Practices from the World's Leading Coaching Programme on Success Intelligence. Hay House: Carlsbad, CA.

A. Barnard & Chris Parker. 2012. Campaign IT! Achieving Success through Communication. Kogan Page: UK. ISBN: 978-0-7494-6420-2

A. Dignen & I. McMaster. 2013. Effective International Business Communication: Build Your Interpersonal Skills in English. Harpercollins: London.

E.A. Taub. 1999. Balance Your Body, Balance Your Life: Total Health Rejuvenation. Pocket Books: New York.

J. Cruise. 2005. The 3-Hour Diet: How Low-Carb Diets Make You Fat and Timing Makes You Thin. HarperCollins: New York.

K. Robinson. 2001. Out of Our Minds: Learning to Be Creative. Capstone Publishing: Chichester, UK.

T. Drake & C. Middleton. 2009. You Can Be as Young as You Think: Six Steps to Staying Younger and Feeling Sharper. Pearson Education: Harlow, UK.

B. Turk. 2008. Life Money: The Proven System for Creating the Money You Need for the Life You Want. Good Times Books: New Delhi.

J. Vitale & B. Hibler. 2006. Meet and Grow Rich. Wiley: Hoeboeken, NJ. ISBN: 978-0-470-04548-5.

A. Griffiths. 2009. Bullet Proof Your Business Now: Essential Advice You Need to Survive Tough Times in Business. Allen & Unwin: Crows Nest, NSW, Australia.

J.C. Maxwell. Everyone Communicates Few Connect: What the Most Effective People Do Differently. 2010. Jaico: Mumbai

S.D. Collins. 2006. Listening and Responding. Cengage Learning India: New Delhi.

S. Corie. 2009. The Art of Inspired Living. Karnac Books: London.

D. Goleman. Emotional Intelligence: Why it Can Matter more than IQ. Bantam Books: New York.

C. Hyland . 2013. Connect through Think Feel Know. Anoma Press: Herts, UK. ISBN: 978-1-908746-75-7.

G. Whitelaw & B. Wetzig. 2008. Move to Greatness. Nicholas Brealey International: Boston, MA. ISBN: 978-1-904838-20-3.

Alan Axelrod. 2009. Winston Churchill, CEO: 25 Lessons for Bold Business Leaders. Sterling Publishers: New York.

Time Life Inc. 2001. Time Life Early Learning Program. Parent's Guide. Educational Technologies Limited. ISBN: 962-8784-26-9. http://www.ETLhomelearning.com

N. Koloff & J. Gitomer. 2004. Wrestling with Success: Developing a Championship Mentality. Wiley: Hoeboken, NJ. ISBN: 0-471-48732-5

Epilogue

Congratulations! You have made this far. Treat yourself with ice creams! Go for the flavor of your choice. If you have not still taken any action, but just read the book, THIS IS THE TIME TO ACT. Start Now!

> Nothing happens until something moves.
>
> —Einstein

> No trumpet sound when the important decisions of our life are made. Destiny is made silently.
>
> —Agnes de Mille

If you took some actions, but gave up somewhere because of some reasons, THIS IS THE TIME TO ACT AGAIN. Remember: *Everything is difficult before it becomes easy.*

> As you begin to take action toward the fulfillment of your goals and dreams, you must realize that not every action will be perfect. Not every action will produce the desired result. Not every action will work. Making mistakes, getting it almost right, and experimenting to see what happens are all part of the process of eventually getting it right.
>
> —Jake Canfield

> Never, never, never, never give up.
>
> —Winston Churchill

If you finished tasting all the "143 licks" of grammar but have not practiced them enough, THIS IS THE TIME TO PRACTICE AGAIN.

> You already know how to succeed. Now all you have to do is take success actions.
>
> —Nikita Koloff & Jeffrey Gitomer

> Victory, Victory at all costs, victory in spite of all terror, victory however long and hard the road may be; for without victory there is no survival.
>
> —Winston Churchill

What flashed in my mind as a small idea has now become a book. Had I not ACTED on this small idea, this idea would have died forever. I too had struggled with my barriers—negative thoughts, not having enough resources, could not arrive at a design, etc.—before seeing the completion of the book. Of course, little by little I have crossed my obstacles. Every missing ingredient came just on time, but only when I started ACTING. It is only by ACTING irrespective of the difficulties, I have seen this book to completion. So, whether you are a minister, administrator, teacher, parent or student, PLEASE ACT. Action is the only way to make things happen!

> Ideas acquire momentum of their own. The Stimulus of a vast concentration of public support is almost irresistible in its potency.
>
> —Winston Churchill

I, as an author, put a lot of effort in collecting the best ideas possible and presented them in the best way I could, along with my valuable experiences. If I have seen this further in this work, it is because and only because that I'm standing on the shoulders of giants. Writing this book is enormously humbling and highly engaging. I appreciate every person who contributed in any way—great or small—to this book. Thank you!

I hope that reading this book has been delightful and helpful to you. I would love to hear from you (even if your writing may have poor grammar). Please send your valuable thoughts, suggestions, criticisms, praises, and directions for my future books to anglo.sphere@yahoo.com.

> Don't take the well-traveled path, the easy trail, the freeway. Slug it out in the trenches, break trails, smash through obstacles, plow through barriers, and bowl over monoliths to accomplish the objective—to communicate in an effective manner.
>
> —Phil Phantom

ABOUT THE AUTHOR

Shalom Kumar Sigworth had been in the Science, Engineering, and Medicine Publishing (STM Publishing) field for over 13 years. He has extensive expertise in Proofreading, Quality Control, Project Management, Stylistic Copyediting, and English language editing of manuscripts from non-native English speakers. He has worked in various publishing media (abstracts, peer-reviewed journals, Books, online databases, and Major Reference Works) and worked for some of the World's prestigious publishers, including Royal Society of London, Elsevier, Taylor and Francis, Oxford University Press, Springer, and Wiley.

Mr. Sigworth is the founder of Anglosphere Education Networks, a private coaching company with the mission of making a variety of English and personal excellence courses *available*, *accessible*, and *affordable* to the general public. Being aware of the ever-increasing need to teach English and job prospects being abounding for English users, he has strategically written this book to bring awareness to the students around the globe. He can be reached at anglo.sphere@yahoo.com or at in.linkedin.com/pub/anglo-sphere/96/334/728/. His blogs can be viewed at www.mind2manifestblogspot.in.